FREEDOM FROM WORK

JACK FECKER

Published by
Hara Publishing
P.O. Box 19732
Seattle, WA 98109
206 775-7868

ISBN: 1-883697-24-7

Library of Congress Catalog Card Number: 96-078297

Manufactured in the United States
10 9 8 7 6 5 4 3 2

Grateful acknowledgment is made for permission granted by Doubleday, a division of Bantam Doubleday Dell Publishing Group, Inc. for portions reprinted from THE HEART AROUSED by David Whyte and by David Wagoner for LOST, copyright 1976.

Supervising Editor: Cherie Tucker
Cover Design: Ron de Wilde
Desktop Publisher: Shael Anderson and Eric Mead

Contents

Acknowledgements

To all my family and friends, I am thankful for your love and support in my life. Specifically, I express my deepest gratitude to:

Jane, my wife – Your encouragement to keep writing and continued vision of this completed book gave me the inspiration I needed. Your passion in living life fully every moment is a constant reminder for me to always go for it!

Lorrie, my daughter – You are a great writer, and you have taught me to persist in working on myself through helping others.

David, my son – You have taught me that I can create what I want without all the struggle.

Jason, my young son – You are teaching me to play more in life by thoroughly enjoying yourself in the moment

Linda Anson – Your special gifts in art therapy served as a catalyst for me to begin writing.

Ron Connor, my friend – You always ask the tough questions at the right time and provide inspiration for our weekly group meetings.

Stan Day, my friend – Though you have had more challenges than anyone should have in three lifetimes, you have always been there for me, and you keep our meetings on track.

Bert Roberts – Your friendship and sense of humor in spite of all life's obstacles have been great assets in my life and in our weekly gatherings.

Charles King – Your love of people and music has been one of the great gifts in my own soul growth. Through song and your friendship, you have helped me to recover those values in my life I had left behind when I was so intent on "earning a living."

* * * * *

The following business partners have greatly assisted me in learning important lessons:

Joe Rutten – You taught me that all work can be fun; that it is all how you "look at it!"

Bob Farrell – You always have been a model for me to stay focused on my goal. That with enthusiasm, it would come to pass!

Bill Keegan – Thank you for teaching me that good taste in food and all of life finds its source in my emotions.

Linda Pressey – You are a lady of great talent and one who encouraged me to be all I could even in the face of great challenges.

Sheila Connor – Thank you for teaching me how to give wonderful seminars integrating both male and female energies.

Gert Popp – In your willingness to share your own life's journey with me, you have been one of my greatest inspirations in learning how to be teachable..

Eva Briggs – Thank you for teaching me that work isn't really about "work," but rather what I learned about life this week!

Mick McHugh – You are a master promoter and also one of the kindest souls I have ever met.

And last but not least, my thanks to two of the most entertaining women on this planet without whose gifts this book would not exist. You have both embodied the meaning of *Freedom From Work* for you invested the best of yourselves in making this project *FUN* instead of work!

Cherie Tucker, my editor – Your impeccable grammar and sense of humor through it all brought out the highest in me.

Sheryn Hara – Thank you for your great vision, patience, and persistence in this project. You are a powerful catalyst for healing change on this planet.

Introduction

Like the word "love," "work" is one of those words that brings up a hundred different emotions that can barely be defined. The term "hard work" has more emotional meaning for me than almost any other in our limited English language. Being raised by a Swiss/German father and a Norwegian mother in North Dakota was an apropos backdrop for my life on the stage of hard work.

I began working at the age of six selling eggs and corn door-to-door and have had several money making work experiences since then such as paper boy, theater usher, gandy dancer (railroad), photographer, toolmaker, draftsman, engineer, candy retailer, singer, night-club owner, advertising salesman, band leader, restaurant owner, public speaker, seminar leader, business consultant, painter, handyman and contractor in that order. Yes, I did have time to play, but once I had reached the age of 26, I was hooked on work.

One of the purposes of any addiction, even "work addiction," is to keep us from our inner journey, from communing with our soul, exploring the unknown. When we have not had an experience of communing with our deepest soul over long periods of time, we, as a people, become lost. That loss of soul has been leaking into every fiber of our society. We experience it in our families, our schools, in our broken relationships, the epidemic of violence and abuse on our children, and the coldness, rigidity and emptiness still the norm in most of our corporate environments.

Thank God, I started to put together and use the following statement about twenty years ago. *It's not important what you do. It is important what you learn about yourself along the way.* My own setbacks, mistakes, failures and disasters have been my own greatest learning experiences and the basis for this book.

When facing the unknown, guidance can be most helpful. Individually, and as a culture, we can be open to guides showing us how to make that inner journey. Guides can build bridges between what we know and what is hidden, the darker side, and then walk those bridges with us through their personal stories, their own soulful journeys. Guides can journey with us through insight, compassion, and yes, especially humor, in exploring the shadows, without the veil of addictions, so we can know ourselves fully. This can enable us to come home to our own souls once again as a culture, remembering the highest and the best of who we really are. This book can be a guide in exploring your own work habits and how they might support or hinder health and balance in other areas of your life.

Addictions in this culture are being revealed at an accelerated rate. Drugs, alcohol, and nicotine are only some of the addictive chemicals being exposed with increasing intensity. Addictions to anger, violence, and sex are also being exposed as destructive to other values we hold, even though at a much slower rate. Yet, the addiction to "work" is most difficult, almost impossible for us to look at as Americans because as a culture, we not only condone and remain in deep denial concerning this addiction, but give it a seat of great honor and credence at every level in our social structures.

To begin to explore our addiction to "work" is to stand on the threshold of inviting us as a culture to explore our soul, the unknown, to take that inner journey as a culture. This, of course, begins with us individually as parents, teachers, ministers, and as workers in the marketplace.

As a culture, we have valued so much and invested everything in our "work" identity. We have bought into the American tribal belief that *we are our work.* Now we are in a time when we are being asked as an entire culture of people to call our Spirits back, to make the inner journey, to bring the soulfulness back into every arena of our lives, our parenting, our homes, our schools, our artistic expressions, and our business ventures with the foundation of being of service to one another from a soul level.

Part of our cultural renaissance at this time, this renaissance of soul, is the revealing of "*work addiction*" for the destructive, camouflaging force that it is. *Freedom From Work* has the courage to explore "work addiction," peeling away the trimmings and trappings of honor, loyalty, and responsibility, bringing it out of the closet of denial.

Decades ago, we never would have considered in business the use of terms such as "vision," "alignment," "trust," "commitment," "intuition." Now it is increasingly normal to be talking with CEO's in terms of vision, alignment, trust. In fact, when I attended a world-wide business conference in Scotland in 1985, leading consultants from the Netherlands in one presentation informed us how they talked with CEO's in major businesses of allowing "love" to operate in the workplace.

Having been in the business realm for 40 years, and much of that time as an entrepreneur, CEO and business consultant, I have seen increasing signs, mostly in the recent decade, of honoring the essence of soul and the foundation of servanthood in all of business. The professionals who are willing to march to this soulful beat are also finding that the natural by-product is financial profitability. Ironic, since it seems the primary fear of most business executives in talking about or bringing any of these truths into leading corporate America is the loss of "profits." However, the universal paradigm that abundance is fast on the heels of authentic service is well-documented by numerous examples in the marketplace.

If allowed, this book can enable you in taking further steps in your own inner journey so you might bring the best of all you are to your own families, your schools, all the places of service in your communities, and especially the workplace.

Enjoy!

Why Work?

Why do I work? Why do I work day after day, year after year? I had never asked myself that question before. It's as if our culture is set up never to ask that question. All I hear is we must keep up with the rest of the world . . . we must raise our standard of living . . . we need more jobs so we can have full employment. Jobs for everyone is of the utmost importance: Work for all, even if no one enjoys the work.

Doing and having has become more important than being. Why? The more questions I ask, the more none of this makes any sense. Questions like:

- *Why do I need to work?*
- *What is retirement?*
- *Do I work to live or do I live to work?*
- *What is job security?*
- *What does standard of living mean?*
- *What is the real difference between work and play?*
- *Should everyone work?*
- *Are there happy people who never work?*
- *What is hard work?*
- *Is work tied to my self-esteem?*

Exploring these questions and many more has been an exciting journey. This book is not about answers so much as exploring the many choices available.

What are our priorities in life? Do they remain constant throughout our lifetime? Is work really the number one priority that we make it?

We now have what we call our productive years, the years when we do the most work. We also have our learning years, then our retirement years. A sliver of thought is creeping into my consciousness telling me that this is all nonsense. What if we replaced our "learning" years with "discovery" years, our "working" years with "discovery" years, and our "retirement" years with "discovery" years? I have observed that there are numerous life examples of great men and women who lived with this "discovery" concept as their priority.

Most people do not live with this concept as a priority. I invite each of us, including myself, to explore and discover how we might make daily choices in thought and deed transitioning to a world of "discovery" from a world of "hard work" and "struggle." The questions nipping on the heels of this invitation are: "How do we get through school?" "How do we pay the bills?" "How do we attain financial security in our retirement years?" Possible creative answers to all these questions and many more are explored in the following pages. One thing you won't find is an attachment to any one process, fix-it solution, or guarantees. Each of us is a unique expression of creative energy. What works for you won't work for anyone else in the exact manner. Your own personal journey is just that, personal. I know that when you are ready, all you need to know will be revealed to you.

All that I have shared in this book are ideas you may want to explore in making up your own journey, never what you "should," "need," or "have" to do. The million-dollar question for many looms, "How do I support, myself, my family, and pay the bills, be responsible, if I don't work?" The answer is easy. If you are willing to allow "discovery" and "exploration" to be your number one priority in life rather than "work," you will inevitably bring into your life all that you need — the opportunities to work in serving existing needs with your unique skills and gifts, and the abundance that will honor that work-service.

I would be less than honest with you if I represented to you that I make this choice 100 percent of the time. That is why I am writing this book, a book that really is continuing with all of us writing our own, individual chapters. Journeys for me are generally more fun when I invite others to come along. You and others like you currently on this quest are going to have a FUN trip!

In my own life, every discovery brings awareness of new choices available. I always have a choice to make decisions based on the new information or keep going in the old direction. My experience is that once I have new information, staying put or repeating the old paths is always more painful than making choices ushering in powerful change. Thankfully, I usually choose to let go of the old paths and explore the new, even though it requires stretching, using new muscles, and is often uncomfortable. Yet these kinds of growing pains are always short-lived, and the rewards are far greater in comparison.

To shift from a place of consciousness enforced by more than 300 years of "work" myths will take some time, and much persistence, and patience. But, if you and I forge on with clear intention, perhaps it can be accomplished with a critical mass in ten to twenty years, or less.

I've got the time and the patience to give to this journey. I invite you again to come along. Old cultural myths die slowly. It will take hard work and much diligence. There I go again, about that "hard work" concept, subtle, and so seductive. Let's try again. It can be the pursuing of our own personal "love vocations" that will end "work" as we know it on this planet. With that thought in mind, it could be absolutely no work at all.

Perhaps it can be Freedom From Work.

Discover

When I was in college taking a difficult physics course, I made an important discovery about my mind, one I really didn't understand until recently. Each day, we were given a difficult problem to solve with the answer to be given in the next class. As long as I was struggling with the problem, I couldn't come up with the answer. After a while, I would just gather all the information needed, then go to sleep. The following morning when I went to my desk immediately upon awaking, I always had the answer easily with no effort. My mind had solved the problem while I was sleeping. I realize now that this was the time when I was tapping into the collective consciousness of the Universe.

Recently I realized that everything I need or want to know has already been answered. All I need to do is look to nature and discover or uncover what this is. The Universe has already provided all the answers. I just need to explore the questions and then get out of my own way in discovering the creative answers.

Discover rather than work.
DIscover rather than create.
Discover rather than invent.
Discover rather than produce.

I had this one backwards from the age of seven, and especially when I became one of the working class.

Addiction to stuff.
Addiction to money.
Addiction to work.

Work produces money, which pays for stuff that we have already acquired on credit, which needs to be kept current, which keeps us entangled in the work force.

So let's start with the work addiction and how to do something about it. Here's one idea. In 1991, 1 started a support group based on the 12-step program of AA. Fifteen people showed up at my home. We called this group "FAMS Anonymous" — Fear About Money Stuff Anonymous. Four of us are still meeting after all these years. After six months, our meetings evolved into a focus around work instead of money and we dropped the 12 steps.

Now we actively support each other in doing the kind of work that gives each one of us the most joy. What a concept! I would not be painting and writing today if it weren't for this group! All of my life, I would find excuses to paint for other people and not for myself.

I loved to paint ever since I was a kid. However. I never thought of painting as a vocation because it was hardly a dignified job and you get dirty every day. Besides, I am a college graduate. Finally, I was living under the old money myth that is common with most Americans, that it's not OK to be paid for enjoying yourself!

Hard work pays the bills, so when I asked my friend, Ron Connor, what I should do after I had gone bankrupt and was out of a steady job, he said, “Do something even if it only pays $5.00 per hour!” The following week I went to work for Ron at $8.00 per hour doing what he loves to do, landscaping. I never worked so hard! I felt I had really earned that $64.00 I brought home the first day. I say “really earned” because I didn't like the work,and I ached all over! He noticed my frustration and asked, “What would you really like to do?” I replied sheepishly, “Paint houses!” to which he responded, “Well, paint my kitchen and cabinets and I'll pay you $500.”

The rest is history. My painting contracting company now accomplishes more than 70 painting jobs each year.

If I were out of work today, I would not look for a job. The first thing I would do is form a support group, other than my family or relatives, to support me in my finding the right work instead of a job. I found that there are no jobs, just lots of work to be done. If I look for a job, I never find one. If I look for work that is already inside of me, just waiting to get out, then I have numerous options.This is exactly what my support group assisted me in discovering: the key word here is “discover.” Our true “work,” that work that will bring you the greatest joy and be of the greatest service to mankind, is already inside every one of *us*. It begins to manifest through our desires and passions for life.

If it's in me, it's in you. I believe each person is a living human treasure embodying the desires and skills that will lead us to the work we are here to accomplish on this planet. For me, it is what I enjoy most . . . what I would do even if I didn't get paid! That is why at this time I am such an excellent painter. I believe painting houses may not be my life's work, but rather part of a larger picture that is unfolding, and one that I am in the process of discovering. Painting is teaching me what it is to be in the moment — the now. I've wondered all my life what "being in the now" felt like and whether or not I could actually cause it to happen!

My present work allows me to examine and discover what present time feels like. Recently, I keep asking, “Why am I painting?” The answer keeps coming back clear and strong, “To discover who you are and what you are here to do in your life.” I can live with that. That's a good reason for me to keep swinging the paint brush!

Non-Attachment To Work

Ron said it last Thursday evening at our weekly meeting, "I want to make my life simpler. I don't need so many things." Our group has now evolved into a time and place where we can be totally honest about our work addictions and the pain it causes in our lives.

It is appearing from our evolution over these years that my attachment to owning things drives me to work. The more attachment, the harder I work. Don't get me wrong. It's OK to have and to work, but I believe it is of the utmost importance to recognize why I do what I do. Only then can I have the freedom to shut it off or turn it on at any given time as opposed to its driving me.

I'm beginning to realize that it is my attachments that cause my pain in life and the working without purpose that gives me disease, dis-ease. When Ron stated, "I don't need so many things," I felt that these get-togethers were all worth it. What a relief to know that I, too, could make my life simpler. What fills up the space when I live a simpler life? Again Ron came up with what he would do with his extra time. He now paints with acrylics on canvas, which is a very creative, healing, and relaxing endeavor for him.

When I look at this activity, I wonder if the addiction to painting, writing, or any of the arts would be preferable to addictions that never express who I really am. I cannot help wondering if artistic endeavors are a step towards non-attachment and away from addiction, one step closer to the authentic me.

I come into this life with nothing and I leave with nothing. The question then becomes, "What do I leave behind?"

My property or my paintings?
My hard work or my artwork?

The Myth of Retirement

"Retirement" was created for people who don't enjoy what they do 100 percent of the time. If workers really were in joy, 100 percent involved with their work, they would be insane to consider retirement. Longevity comes from, and is a by-product of, joy, doing what you love.

Can you imagine successful artists quitting what they love at 65 so they could play golf or go fishing. No! They simply continue polishing their craft, and their art becomes even more successful. "Retirement" was created by government and big business to keep people on jobs that they would not do otherwise if they weren't getting paid and the big carrot "Retirement" weren't being dangled at the end of a long period of drudgery, sometimes 20, 30, 40 years later.

One day while working as an engineer at Boeing, my supervisor came up to me. We had come to know each other fairly well. Quite candidly, he stated, "Jack, quit now before it's too late. Once you put in enough years, you won't be able to leave. I'm a good example of what

I'm talking about." My stay with Boeing lasted only six more months. I never received my five-year pin and to this day, I am thankful for his wise remarks. One year later I was in business for myself beginning more than 34 years of entrepreneurial adventures. I never looked back.

We as a society have not only accepted the myth of "retirement," but have made it into a Badge of Honor symbolizing our loyalty: "I have been loyal to my business/organization for 30 years now, so I can retire from work and live out the rest of my life in peace with good conscience." The big drawback is that in most cases, that "rest of my life" lasts from six months to three years, a pretty risky badge to wear!

I was over at a friend's home recently when he mentioned that his next-door neighbor was retiring from Boeing the following week. I thought it might be worthwhile to interview him and find out just how it felt for him. I never got the chance. He died one day after he retired.

Perhaps a healthier timeline would be that we are just getting to know ourselves at age 60 and producing our best works after 65. The evidence is out there if we choose to look at it. My own father, at age sixty-five, moved to Seattle and began looking for work. His comfort zone was to work. He had decided that if he couldn't find work, he would go back to North Dakota where he was already in great demand as a butcher. (I wonder where I inherited my own desire to work hard?)

My dad lied about his age just to work at a large steel plant picking up scraps in the yard. Eventually he became foreman of a pit crew pouring steel at age 65 while they assumed he was 55. He worked there for ten years retiring at the supposed age of 65 when he was really 75. Confused yet?!

My dad eventually went to work for me in my restaurants. Anyone who knew him believed he did his best work after age 70. My father retired at 97 years old because this was the first year he wasn't able to pass the Washington driver's exam. He died at the wonderful age of 101 years old, having kicked up his heels on the dance floor at a grandiose 100th birthday party one year earlier.

The seduction of all myths is that we usually don't wish to look at them, at least not too closely or for very long. If I have invested 30 years at some activity and it has been boring or unfruitful for me, the last thing I want to admit is that I've been living a myth. I would much rather be justified and succumb to the social peer pressure that what I am doing is important, powerful, and worthwhile, even though I have ruined my health, never learned how to live in the moment, perhaps have never contributed fully to healthy relationships, and have assisted in destroying our beautiful environment.

Is "retirement" worth all this?

Work Addiction

Why do I need to work? I have come to the conclusion that I am a work addict. I am noticing that this work addiction is unlike nicotine or alcohol addiction in that they tend to be in the minority. My theory is that work addiction defines the majority of our population over the age of 21 — perhaps as high as 75 to 80 percent of the working class.

We call this the "working class." It's funny. We graduate from our high school class or college class and right away, without any significant period of time, we join the working class. We have been well prepared in that all our parent models and school training sets us up to be hooked to a major addiction that almost no one wants to look at.

What is going on here? If you want to be an outcast from the working class, just try admitting you are a writer, artist, dancer, or inventor. Why is so much value placed on a working profession and vocation that allows little free thinking, almost no invention, and no creativity? My guess is that when I am addicted to something, I try to get everyone around me to partake in my addiction so I don't have to look at my situation and then I won't feel so bad. Conversely, if I am the only one addicted to work in a family of free thinkers, so called artists and the like, I might feel out of place.

The work myth in this country is out of control. Look how many people you know who never take a vacation and wear that as a badge of honor. I have noticed more people are working longer hours now than 20 years ago, and yet it was predicted that by the year 2000, the majority of us would have more free time. But what are we to do with three to four more days off per week?!

Over ten years ago, I decided to take a week off from work with nothing planned. A full week of spontaneity! After a few days experiencing my "uncomfort zone" of uncertainty, I began to have a pretty good time doing everything on the spur of the moment. It was fun! Why haven't I tried it again?

A recent article in the *Reader's Digest* entitled, "Are Americans Working Too Hard?" states that factory employees in the United States work two and one-half months more per year than their German counterparts; that's an additional 430 hours!

When I am addicted, I create situations to feed my addiction, and I make up excuses to keep the cycle going. The biggest excuse for work addiction in our society is called "standard of living," and our elected officials really know how to milk that one. In order to maintain our "standard of living," we must produce. Produce what? Stuff. . . things. . . .*more stuff!*

We can't dispose of what we produce now in a healthy manner for our planet. Why on earth do we need more stuff! Perhaps once I do admit I am addicted, I can be aware of what is going on and make some changes. What will it take for the workers of this great country to wake up and at least acknowledge that this work addiction is in epidemic proportions.

It can start with me. I can start by forgiving all the people who don't work, who don't produce. Of course, as in nature, these folks possess a beauty all their own! I can start by being aware of my own feelings when I am not working.

I can look at life as something other than mostly work, but primarily a time for discovery. I can then devote more time for this discovery. I may be able to start with only a few minutes a day and then gradually progress to a conscious awareness of exploration and discovery for most of my day. I can go to places where discovery is easiest, the library, woods, mountains, the beach.

Am I on this planet to work or to discover? My guess is as we expand the hours in the day where we can discover what is important, we will begin to recover what we have sacrificed as individuals, families, and communities on the altar of "work."

I Must Earn It!

I wonder if the majority of my "work" is for the purpose of earning a living. On a scale of one to ten, I would say my "work to earn a living" is probably around an eight. What about you?

The world is already set up to give us the abundance it is pouring forth. Yet, even though I know on one level everything is there for me, I continue to labor under the pressures of needing to earn it, work for it, toil and sweat for it. My wife, Jane, and I had moved into our first home back in 1984. Because she and I both love music, having a piano was something we had talked about often. However, being the thrifty budgeteer that I am, I made certain she knew up front that we wouldn't for a long while be able to afford a grand piano. Then, of course, being the visionary that she is, Jane reminded me that if we let go of the how, we could open our lives up to what we wanted — the piano! Well, it didn't cost me anything to do that, so I went along with holding the vision. Meanwhile, Jane held the very specific vision of a cherry wood, German-made grand piano. Yeah, right!

Within one month, some dear friends who had been going through a separation, came to us asking if we would consider storing their grand piano in our home while they relocated. We had not even mentioned to them our desire for a piano. Of course, we obliged and one day the piano movers showed up on our doorstep with this grand piano. Now this was no ordinary piano! This was a cherry wood, German-made grand piano, and a highly valued antique over 100 years old! Of course, I gave Jane the satisfaction of reminding me that focusing on the vision instead of the how makes all the difference. We had this lovely piano in our home for an entire year, at which time our friends had prepared their own new home for it to go, and we had saved enough money to buy our own new piano.

If I had not let go on some level of needing to "earn" the money to have a piano, I could have missed out on this lovely addition to our lives for over a year. "Earning a living" is a concept that has permeated our language, our thoughts, and our feelings. As a male in this society, I deeply believe I must work even harder to support my family. Even if I didn't have a family, I am fairly certain I would work just as intensely to support an imaginary family dictated by sheer habit and the work ethic so deeply embedded in my makeup.

The old memories were recorded in our American cultural genes a long, long time ago that for my family to survive into the next generation, I must work to earn a living. There is part of me that remains convinced that if I do this, I will have succeeded in my lifetime. Life insurance relies on these feelings. I have watched many men in our society work their whole lives, set up a retirement nest egg, and then die at age 65 or soon thereafter, because they are no longer needed and their family has been taken care of.

Is man's primary function to work and keep the family name alive from generation to generation? In our society, I am considered successful if I provide a high standard of living. Perhaps while I am still living, I need to change my thoughts from "high standard of living" to "quality of life."

My Thoughts Are the Foundation

Yesterday, I repaired a back deck on a home for a client. All the support timbers were rotten at the bottom where they touched the dirt and cement and had to be replaced. It was what society calls hard work as the deck had to be supported while the beams were being replaced to prevent the whole deck from crashing down on me.

Sometimes my thoughts need replacing. Especially the ones that support my whole structure. If I look close, I can see where there is dry rot. It's not easily seen from the surface, but when I probe and poke around, I can find it. My whole structure is in danger — my health, my prosperity, and my peace of mind. When I catch it early, I can prevent a complete collapse.

Some basic thoughts, such as, the world is a not a friendly place, or my government is not taking care of me, or people are just down right stupid, creep in after reading the newspaper or watching TV. In each case, I'm talking about myself since everything out there is a mirror of what's going on inside, and these thoughts start the rotting process from the inside out. If caught early like the dry rot on the deck, the structure will not fall. If I can repair it with care, I will return to a safe and sound condition, mentally and physically.

My thoughts are the foundation of my human condition.

A More Powerful Thought

Can I move my thoughts on a conscious level from a less powerful thought to a more powerful thought? If this has value to me, what are some of the steps? How can I move from the competitive to the cooperative and ultimately to the creative mind? Here is one discovery I made in the last few years. When I play tennis, I most often beat myself when I play to beat my opponent. When I think, "I will play creative tennis rather than competitive tennis," I find I most often win, especially when I hold that thought throughout the entire match. Perhaps I am simply more at ease.

It appears that the competitive mind attracts more money while the cooperative mind attracts more friends. However, it is the creative mind that gives me the greatest peace of mind and tremendous joy in my work. If this is so, which of the following is more powerful?

To learn?
To invent?
To discover?

When I am working for someone else as in a large company, it is possible that I can be learning all the time. I can even invent, but more often than not, there is little time or space allowed for real discovery in today's work culture. My times of quality discovery come when I am just being, being in the present. When I am living under someone else's deadlines, I find I am propelled into the future and anxiety sets in. To me, the ultimate discovery is: What have I learned about myself in any given time?

To discover who I really am requires major awareness on my part. How can I quantify this? For myself, when I ask another person, "What have you learned about yourself since we last met?" I am asking, "What did you discover about you?" When the answer flows out of that person, I receive a 100-fold bolt of energy emanating from that being. When they tell me what they have learned or invented, I receive a much lesser energy. A comparison would be the difference in the energy I get when a friend is telling me about what he loves to do rather than what he has to do.

How does this all relate to our work situation? If I can work where I can discover, rather than learn, I now can choose what kind of work I will be involved with. I now understand why I have often said, "If I went back to college or started all over again, I would take astronomy and anthropology," both discovery subjects. Discovery appears to generate more powerful thoughts, more powerful energy, and, therefore, seems to be a more powerful state of mind.

The late R. Buckminster Fuller, our most profound inventor of this era (the Geodesic Dome), was involved for most of his life in discovering the geometry of our planet Earth, which in turn is the geometry of the universe. Einstein was involved in discovery of how light and matter operate in our universe. Imagine what our world and social environments could be if only we were taught in our schools that it is more worthwhile to "discover" than simply to learn some rote skill just so we might earn a living.

Learned skills are fine and they often assist us in the art of "discovery." However, shifting our priorities from learning or mastering skills to the art of "discovery" seems to be a more powerful conscious move.

Do I Work to Live or Live to Work?

Both! I have noticed that in our American society, we have this fantasy with "the productive years." I prepare for the productive years for some 20 years of my life from age 6 to 26. I am productive for 40 years, supposedly reaching my peak in my 40's and 50's, and then it's down hill from there all the way until I am 6-feet under!

Perhaps the most "productive" years are ages 0 to 6, and age 65 to 100. It appears in the case of our great thinkers that age was irrelevant in terms of their productivity. For most of us, me included, perhaps the most wasted time or least productive time is from the ages 25 to 65. That is when we seem to work at "work," the kind of activity that may not necessarily benefit others or the planet, but only ourselves. This is the "getting time" of our lives. Let's take a closer look at this phenomena.

When I was four, all I needed to be was:

Full of Wonder	*Artistic*
Curious	*Forgiving*
Loving	*Close to Nature*

Playful	*Healthy*
Creative	*Imaginative*
Fulfilled	*Childlike*
Accepting	*Honest*

Why is it when I get older, these become the virtues I aspire to rather than actually live? If I demonstrated them actively at four years of age, did I somehow lose them along the way while I was working hard?

Whatever isn't used, atrophies. Something must take its place. As I grew older, I got subtle messages from home, school, role models, etc., that wonder, curiosity, playfulness, creativity, discovery, exploration were not necessarily important qualities to develop as you became an adult. Eventually, I began to replace them with:

Worry	*Guilt*
Greed	*Anxiety*
Work	*Compromise*
Have to's	*Lack of Time*
Fear of Change	*Reality*

Discovery: When I was four, I was more in the present, living in the moment. Now that I am "grown up," I am often seduced to live in the past and in the future instead of in the present moment. I notice that I have traded in a goodly portion of my "wonder" and "curiosity" for guilt and anxiety.

Can I choose to live in the moment? Can my emotions now be joy? If so, then I can be all the things I need to be. My goal is each moment to practice recapturing the four-year-old Self in me that brings the wonder, curiosity, playfulness, and childlikeness to all of my life.

Perhaps *Now I Can Be All I Need to Be!*

When I Don't Have Work

Yesterday I discovered that when I am in turmoil or going through some ordeal, things can happen revealing new ideas and information to me. Yesterday I didn't have a job. It was three weeks past the time for our house payment and no money in sight. I felt down and empty even though it was my birthday. I went and spent two hours at the library.

At the library, I discovered how to look up books and titles on the computer. A nice lady came by and gave me assistance. I now feel I have access to a vast arena of knowledge given to me just spending a few hours at the library.

Here, on a day when I was feeling useless because I had no work, I ended up rediscovering Emerson, Eric Hoffer, Bucky Fuller, and discovering Studs Turkel for the first time — a reputable bunch of thinkers! I found that they all had something to say on the subject of work, but I could not find any complete books on the subject of "not working."

So I'm still asking the question, "Why do we work?" as opposed to create, invent, and discover? The answers I get are, "so we can eat," "so we can have a roof over our heads." If I were uninterested in exploring further, this answer might suffice. However, a more powerful, higher thought could be to learn about manifesting food and shelter through greater creativity and discovery. What a world we could create if we were willing 100 percent of the time to explore and pursue our desires, our needs and wants, experiencing a life with no limitations, living in a continual realm of unlimited possibilities.

Why is it in the past few years, I needed to be working, laboring and painting houses to eat and provide shelter? My guess is so I could spend more energies exploring and discovering what I have shared in this book, the essence of the highest form of "work," and its relationship to how we fully live our purpose on this planet.

I like painting houses enough to continue, and I am starting to feel "secure" about this work. One of the dangers of "work" is that when it becomes out of balance, we can sacrifice many of our values, our relationships and even parts of ourselves on the altar of responsible work, expecting it to give us many things, including a false sense of security. Often "work" can seduce me to rely on a specific paycheck, an employer or occupation just so I can experience "certainty." I can be tempted to trade being true to myself, my gifts and passions, and avoid looking at what is not working in a job, or in my life, for the security blanket of "certainty." This way I can avoid experiencing any dark shadows that might surface, fears of not being good enough, or feelings of inadequacy and uselessness when I am being challenged to "be" instead of "do."

Someone has to paint houses. Then again, maybe not. Maybe painting houses was invented just so we could put more people to work! Perhaps what I am doing is not so secure after all if enough people figure out that what I do is not needed and discover an easier, more efficient way to do this job.

It's like the current status of the lumber industry. Because of the state of our resources, we do not need the lumberjacks in the same manner as we did years ago. If you dare, ask yourself, "Am I in a dying business, craft, trade, vocation?" If the answer is "yes," then you probably are on the doorstep of a great inner journey, exploring new rooms of your creativity, passions, dreams, and skills that in turn will lead you into a richer, fuller experience of your unique mission in being here.

Wonder — Wonder Has Gone Out of the Workplace

Has the a sense of wonder gone out of our lives? Has wonder gone out of the workplace?

Briane Swimme in his *Canticles of the Universe* explains how we are the only species in the universe that gawks. Only we stop and look at the wonder in nature. We must allow ourselves to gawk and to provide environments for gawking!

My thought on this subject takes me back 200 or 300 years ago when we were much closer to nature and the elements. Our education integrated an understanding of nature because, among other reasons, schools and buildings of learning were situated in areas abundant in wildlife and nature. At present, many of our schools are surrounded by concrete and chain-link fences with no animals or foliage in sight.

It appears the further away we move from nature, wonder, and discovery, the more violent we become as a culture. This is not the only contributor to violence in our culture by any means. However, I do believe one of the ways we can heal the wounds that contribute to the violence is to create places in our homes, schools, and our communities for our children to explore and gawk at nature. We can teach them by ourselves learning anew the simple act of wonder and discovery in every area of our lives.

Why would I get excited to go to a place of learning where all they do is lecture, where discovery is placed on the back burner? So what happens when we get to the work place? Wonder is gone, discovery has disappeared, and what we were able to learn and memorize becomes a mere servant.

Most of us work in environments that are stale, where there is no provision for wonder or discovery and, therefore, most of our creativity and invention muscles atrophy. Any worker's natural abilities to be an entrepreneur are smothered in this setting, and often are suffocated altogether.

Are our work places mirrors of our school places, or is it the other way around? It just might serve us better to once again have one room school houses close to nature. Maybe we were on to something without really knowing it. Many of our great thinkers came out of that setting. These were individuals known not so much for their intellectual knowledge as for their developed skills of wondering, discovery, and exploration. It was this sense of wonder that opened the unlimited possibilities of learning and universal knowledge to them, and in turn to us through their model of discovery.

This sense of "wonder" is one of the most valuable legacies we can leave to our children.

Work and Relationships

There are jobs looking for people and people looking for jobs. Why is it they seldom meet?

Finding a job is like finding a partner — when I stop looking, the relationship comes into my life. It must be the same with jobs. When I'm intensely looking for the right person in my life, I tend to be very critical about everyone I meet. Consequently, the right person doesn't reveal herself to me. She's too tall, too skinny, too fat, too demanding and wants my money!

When I look for the right job, I become critical and the job doesn't find me. I'm overqualified, it's too big, too many hours, too little pay, or too demanding! I have never found the perfect relationship. But I have developed good relationships by focusing on them, giving attention. There must be more to a job than just the technical aspects as there is more to a relationship than fixing up the house, paying the bills, and feeding the family.

So I evolve a job as I evolve a relationship. I can love my job and love my relationship or I can hate my job and hate my relationship. Sometimes I see people hating their job, but loving their relationship. It must make a difference where they focused their attention. Jobs are as plentiful as relationships.

I was told long ago that there are two major areas for personal growth to occur — being in the market place and being in relationships. It appears to me that it is essential to discover and learn all I can about these two areas while I am living. Even if it looks scary and looks like I will fail, I must get into the market place in some way and I must be in a relationship with my body, mind and soul — with my heart and with my emotions.

If it doesn't appear that either are out there, I start by helping out my neighbor. There is always something that needs doing. This path just might lead me to my life's work and my life's companion.

Job Security

Never, never, never go for job security unless I want a slow death! . . . one of my discoveries.

Right now it appears that job security leads to sameness, leads to boredom, leads to anxiety, leads to slow death. On the other side, so-called job insecurity leads to anxiety, leads to thinking, leads to creativity, leads to discovery.

Twenty-five years ago I heard, "Security comes from knowing I can take care of myself." It then appears my security is in direct proportion to taking responsibility for myself. That includes my work. No one else has anything to do with my work. If I acquire a job, I am filling a need out there with my own talents and skills. No one has anything to do with it but me. I, therefore, cannot look to the government to provide me with a job or any company to provide me with work. It's up to me.

I have come to the final conclusion that *there are no jobs,* only work that needs doing. My job security comes from discovering what needs exist in the marketplace, and giving my service to filling those specific needs. If I become talented in doing a certain job, I will have an endless supply of work, if I want it.

If I find some things don't need doing, like cutting more trees down or building more cars, why would I go into that line of work? Maybe I can discover a greater need. Why do I stick with old, established work that does not really cry out for doing? Maybe because it appears there is job security in that line. If I really take a look at what needs are out there without my blinders on, it is mind boggling!

It is time I open my eyes and look at what is before me. I think we have mined enough metal, built enough cars, and cut enough trees for now. There was a time when that was what the world needed, and we created jobs and work to meet those needs. The question today is what are the needs before me; in what ways does the world and its peoples need to be nourished and nurtured?

My job security lies in the answer to this question!

Moving from a "Working" Person to a "Learning" Person

What is a "working" person?

All my models of how to be when I grew up were working persons. The best working models worked the hardest, put in the most hours at work, and brought home the money so we could eat, keep warm, and go to school. My logic told me that if I worked harder, my family would be happier. Only the hard workers and those who suffered the most would get into Heaven. This was my definition of a "working" person.

What is a "learning" person? My model of a learning person was one who learned as much as he could, went to college, if possible, and then out into the world to work until he could work no more. What I didn't understand was that when the working started, the struggle between working and learning also began. How much time and effort do I now devote to each one? I didn't have any clue as to what this new model would look like. I still struggle with this concept in my everyday life.

What I hear in 1994 is that the organizations that will survive the longest must become "learning organizations."

The only problem with this is that when the work load drops off, the learning stops. It's the first thing to be dropped from the budget. Perhaps if I am to become a learning person, I must set my priorities differently with a balance of working and of learning. It appears to me that I don't function very well without the two side by side. I do know that when I am open to increased learning, I usually end with my work becoming easier with more time for leisure.

There is a big difference between working at my trade and learning the skills of that trade and working at serving the needs of others while learning about myself.

> *"When I am using my talents to fill the needs of the world, I am doing what God wants."*
>
> Albert Schweitzer

> *"When I am using my strengths to fill the needs of my neighbor, I am in harmony."*
>
> Jack Fecker
> Speech, 1976

My evolution in this area has developed from working at Boeing building airplanes, to owning and operating a series of restaurants, to helping people fix up and paint their homes. Of course, when I was at Boeing, I believed wholeheartedly that building airplanes was the highest calling and definitely the most important job. My parents agreed. This was job security — high salary, great bonuses, vacations, and a funded retirement.

Helping others paint and repair their homes now gives me the highest feeling of joy with job security at 100 percent, as every house I see needs some attention! The best part is that while I am working on these houses, I also have the time to work on my own inner home, my soul self. Perhaps I could be learning about myself while working at a big factory or for some large corporation. For me, the concepts of serving others and learning about myself go hand in hand. Perhaps this is my natural state of being. If I had not experienced these other jobs, I doubt I would have discovered this balance of learning and working.

I wonder if individuals with an attitude of serving others naturally expose themselves to the discovery of who they are. The question I ask myself is, why didn't I start out with the attitude of serving others and save myself all this time and painful experiences? Perhaps becoming who I am along with this discovery requires working both sides of the road. Otherwise I would never know when I am close to being on the road. At least in my case, I have shifted from being a "working" person to a "learning" person. Here the road feels much less bumpy. It's such a relief to no longer be driving on the shoulder!

Living in Present Time

When I know, when I co-create, when I trust, *the work somehow gets done.*

If I let go and the work flows through me, I experience an abundant flow of energy that is difficult to stop. I can stop it by being anxious or afraid. I can stop it by feeling guilt. These emotions, these judgments, transport me out of living in the present moment wherein lies my unlimited source of energy.

When I worked for Boeing as an engineer, I felt guilt most of the time. Am I good enough? Am I making my parents proud of me? I should like and enjoy what I am doing. When I worked for myself as an owner of a chain of restaurants, I was mostly anxious and worried about the future. Will I reach my goals? Will the advertising work? Will my employees stay with me?

How do I get into present time when I am in that kind of life?

What is the answer?

If I could do it over again with the present system we have, I would recommend a few years practice of present-time living before entering the working class, married class, or owning class replete with mortgages and credit cards. This "practice" would come from service to humanity with rewards being the emotions we receive from contributing our time and energies. It would be a time of discovery with two years of service anywhere on the planet using our talents and strengths to help others where the need is greatest.

This time of contribution could also give me the tools to look at my world, my fellow man, and myself with different, wiser, more compassionate eyes. Most of all, I would have the practice of living day to day, hour to hour and closer to the present time, an exercise practiced little by most on this planet.

How many cultures have retirement plans, medical plans, IRA's, and insurance protecting against the fall-out of most any event, all anxiety-producing. This idea would have some effect on breaking my cycle of working as I know it today. It could just cause me to think differently about work.

Mission — Our Unique Path

I spent the weekend with an old friend in Vancouver, B.C. He has quit his employment of 10 years with the same company and has not been working during the past year. He shared how it has been a most enjoyable year.

He was part owner in a manufacturing company. When I asked what his work would be in the future, he said he didn't know. When I inquired what he would do if money was not an issue, he confessed that he would like to be Jacques Cousteau. He went on to describe with vivid excitement how he would conduct field trips for others through estuaries, (bird sanctuaries). Without hesitation, I urged him, "Do it!" It was obvious that it would give him great joy. Yet, he is still struggling with his choice.

Question: Why is it so difficult for us humans to find our mission — our place in what seems like a giant puzzle? There are many ways to describe it: To do what God wants, to be who we really are, to contribute to the whole of mankind. People who have explored and live their mission in life, or their "birth vision" referred to by James Redfield in *The Tenth Insight,* appear fulfilled and joyful, not just on the outside, but inside as well. They seem to radiate an inner contentment and a quite contagious energy.

I was told many times to find a need and fill it, and to match the need with my God-given talents. Which do I find first — my talents or the need? Maybe neither. Perhaps there is no answer to this dilemma. How does one find his or her purpose in life that gives great joy and knowing?

In my own case, I believe as I move toward the work that gives me the greatest joy, I am getting closer. If I go with the flow of the river of life, I seem to be happier. I believe every one of our dreams, our desires, wishes, are there for the purpose of being a guidemap from our Higher Self to our conscious self leading us into our life mission. Whenever I have tried or forced anything, I end up creating more difficulty or pain in my life, but when I follow what I enjoy, what I love, my life gets easier.

How do I know if I am on the right path? I can look for signs to see if this is my mission path. I don't believe there is a right path as then there would be a wrong one, and no one is on the wrong path. There seem to be many choices available in any given moment, all of which can lead us to the very Highest of who we are.

What do the signs look like? What do they say? How big or small are they and do they point in a direction? Some of my signs are health — how do I feel?

Peace of mind — how anxious or guilty do I feel? Prosperity — do I worry about money or having things?

It appears it is more about how I feel, what I perceive, and little to do with facts, logic, or what others think or do. It becomes a very personal, individual experience and journey that cannot be reduced to mere words. I will know when I know, and I am the only one traveling on my path. I have just discovered how unique each one of us is on this planet. There are no two paths or missions the same! Some similarities, some likeness, but when examined, I am totally alone, and yet feel a part of a much greater, unlimited purpose.

This is why I say there are no jobs. There is just your work, your purpose that you individually create and invent, sometimes within the framework of an existing organization. Maybe my path is my mission. How do I stay on it and know? My own intuition, the wizard inside me who is the seer, will be with me at every turn on the path. It has always been my guide in the past and will continue to be in the future as I give it credence and listen quietly.

How I Feel About Having Work

I am now gainfully employed. I have three to four jobs that will last for three weeks. I feel secure. I feel less pressure. Too much work, *pressure*. No work, *pressure*. Why does this pressure thing have such an emotional grip on my life?

Why can't I just live day to day with an even amount of low pressure? Could it be my "I wants?" Or could it be what *"I must have?"* "Have to's" create more pressure in my life than "I wants." Some of the old "I wants" have changed to "have to's." *Example*: From radio to black and white TV to color, to big screen to cable. Now, I *have to* pay $24.00 per month to have TV cable.

It's the same with the telephone, the washer and dryer, the dishwasher, the car, the two-car garage, and the two and one-half bathroom house. As more and more "wants" are changed to "have to's," the pressure builds.

Is a more simple life OK in this society? Where is the pressure coming from? It appears on the surface that it is self-imposed. If I didn't self-impose this pressure, would it be OK to be without work, or would I still have pressure to get a job? I don't know which comes first, the "have to's" in my life or having work to do? I think they feed off each other, and it becomes a treadmill that goes around with no rest.

Where is the balance? I have been accused of settling for less or wanting too much. To be balanced is to walk a fine line between the two. How do I achieve this?

It must take practiced awareness to find where the center is located in my life. I am the only one who can find that center. I will discover it as I tune out others and listen internally. I must also pay attention to others and listen externally as well. I want to listen and be present in both realms, not just one or the other.

There are no answers, only questions. Can I live my whole life with questions and no answers? Perhaps, if I can give up my need to know, to be certain about anything. It's OK to live a life of not knowing and question everything that goes on around me. I believe I can *BE*. I can be centered with only the questions echoing in my mind.

Immediate Rewards For Work

Yesterday, I finished a three-day painting job. I always write an invoice at the end and hand it to the owner of the home. I expect to get paid when I complete the job. This accomplishes two things: 1) I receive my reward immediately on completion of my work, and 2) I can go out and buy something for myself, which gives me a feeling of satisfaction.

I like immediate rewards for a job well done. I knew we had done a terrific job in painting the three rooms on this specific job. The client was a little disappointed with some cracks still showing in the ceiling. This was not our responsibility as the home was already 60 years old. I would have liked to have heard some praise or one little comment of acknowledgment that our work was satisfactory. However, none was forthcoming.

The client then asked if he could mail us the check since he was a little short on funds. "Uh, oh, here's trouble." were my next thoughts. I responded that I would like to get the check now even if he needed to postdate. He then wrote it out for today. I went to his bank and cashed it on my way home. I hesitated, but then thought how important it is to be paid when finishing a project.

In most jobs I've had, like most people in this country, I was paid on a two-week basis, whether I accomplished anything or not. Once in a while, I would receive a raise which was definitely exciting. But this generally occurred only once a year. Now I have that same rush of excitement every week, sometimes twice a week! I even request one-third down before starting the work so I can have two excitements per job. When the client is satisfied and comments on the work, this is an extra bonus. Often they write a letter of recommendation affirming their satisfaction.

Wouldn't it be exciting if all work could be this way? It probably could be if more people could live through the uncertainty of not having a salaried paycheck coming in every month. To me, there is security knowing I can take care of myself. I don't depend on anyone for my paycheck. If a client gives me a bad time or holds off payment, I don't work for them anymore. There are thousands of job opportunities out there and each one needs help in painting or fixing up their home or business. One old adage states, "Our rewards are in exact proportion to our contribution." It's always nice when they are within hours of each other!

What I Fear Today Is My Next Assignment!

My fear today is that I won't have enough time to do all the things I want to do and I won't have enough money to buy the things I want. Time and money are energy conversions. With more and more energy, more things occur in a given time. With more and more energy, more of my energy is converted to money. If I allow my energy to wane, I could have less time and money. Perhaps if I focus on increased energy, then I will have increased time and money in my life. Maybe if I increase my energy 100 percent, I will double my time and my money income.

Outflow equals income. How can I raise my energy by a factor of 100 percent? This would be a solution to a problem I have set up. Do I need a solution or do I already have one? Is it OK to have the energy I am blessed with at this moment? If I can accept what I have and love what I already possess, then I will have all I want.

I now accept and love the energy that I have at this time. Always when I return to the moment, it follows that all the fear fades away. I am enough. I have enough time and enough money in the present and I also have all the energy I will ever need in the present. My next assignment is now a past assignment.

Can all fears be handled so easily? Perhaps it's a matter of putting them on paper so the mind can view them from a distance. What a marvelous tool mankind has invented, the projecting of our thoughts onto a flat surface away from the brain. Thoughts are projected outward and then formed into word pictures and brought back into our brain in a much more orderly fashion than its initial transmission. Perhaps decisions are best made by viewing our thoughts from a non-attached position once removed. It appears the non-attachment comes from releasing the energy around a thought.

It follows that I must make it OK to have any thought, worry, fear, or problem in my life. OK-ness and non-attachment are my guardians and warriors that handle fear. Living in the now, the moment, is where God is. God is Love. Love is the ultimate destroyer of fear if I can but approach the fear.

It appears the road can start with OK-ness and non-attachment and then move into "now," the present moment, which appears to be the ultimate safe place.

Values vs. Job Security

R. Buckminster Fuller once said, "There is no joy equal to that of being able to work for all humanity and doing what you are doing well." How can I work for all humanity and be in the business community? A business is where you receive compensation for your work and it also involves employment of others in this endeavor.

I keep thinking of Anita Roddick and her Body Shop enterprise located now in every major city around the world. My wife, Jane, and I met Anita in Scotland at a world-wide business conference in 1987. She is an authentic example of a business *demonstrating environmentally-sound* principles on a large scale. I would like to believe that all business could provide a great service and also work in harmony with environmental and other values in the process.

It appears that many large businesses are in the business of staying in business even if it means going against the flow of preserving or contributing to a healthy way of life. Values are tossed out the window to secure the continuance of a paycheck or the fulfillment of a business agreement.

In my own case, there have been various times in my life when I did everything I could just to stay in business, to maintain my demand in the marketplace just so I could maintain a steady flow of income into my bank account. I wonder if job security is all it is cracked up to be? Job security at any cost appears to be the message we pass on to our children. I have been known to change or bend my values and my priorities when my job security was at stake.

Where is the joy of working for all mankind in this scenario? There is not much joy in altering my values to become more secure. When I do, I harm or compromise all of humanity in the process. Perhaps I can teach my children that service to mankind takes precedence, including relationships with my family and friends. Job security comes in far behind. My experience has been that the money comes when I am living my priorities in a healthy order. The sad thing is that the money also comes to individuals who have their values misconstrued, when everything is sacrificed on the altar of greed to obtain it.

I wonder if *values* rather than job security could be placed at the top of our educational system. It would be incumbent upon each of us as parents, teachers, and all community leaders to support this model so we might present it in powerful ways to the impressionable minds of our children. Most of what I heard when I was growing up was job security ... job security . . . . job security. Not much of a legacy.

Work to Feel Safe

Why do I feel safe when I work? Why do I feel safe when I have a job? I feel safe when I have a job coming up, but I feel less safe when I am working. It might be I am contemplating the excitement of a new challenge and the unanswered questions of how much money I might make for my services, and how much service will I be allowed to give to this job?

What I just realized is I have a job every single day whether I know it or not, whether I get paid or not. What I do each day is preparation for what I will do tomorrow when a new opportunity is presented. I remember an old saying by Rudyard Kipling:

What you do when you don't have to, determines what you will be when you can no longer help it.

When I read a book, watch a video or movie, talk to a friend, or just meditate, it is never a waste of time as long as I focus on what I can learn from that experience. Perhaps I can feel safe with *only* what I *learn* about myself.

From 1970 to 1975, my most vivid memories of what I learned about myself was my experience in Toastmasters, an organization designed to give members confidence in public speaking. What seemed like wasted time writing, practicing, and giving speeches on seemingly frivolous subjects was one of my greatest learning periods. I did not receive any pay for my study and work. Years later, I could see the tremendous benefit from that experience, but it was difficult to imagine at the time.

When I look back, I can recall with vivid emotion my life's *learning* experiences, yet can barely remember my working experiences! If I feel so much better about my learning experiences, why then do I put so much time and effort into getting a job so I can feel safe? Perhaps the idea of *feeling safe* is not so important in my life. Perhaps I can substitute *trust* in the place of feeling safe and live a much more rewarding existence.

Why do I feel safe when I have a job? This is the manner in which I was trained. It is now up to me to *learn to trust.* It follows that no job has the power to make me feel one way or the other.

What I do when I don't have to, determines what I will be when I can no longer help it.

Opportunity

"Opportunities To Learn The Business"

This is the heading I put on our ads whenever I was advertising for individuals to come work for me. It was always placed in the "Job Opportunities" section of the *Seattle Times*. My own learning experience in hiring help was mostly a flop as long as I was intent in offering a "job" to someone. One day when placing an ad for a much-needed position, "Someone to Assemble Sandwiches in my restaurant, Sandwich Maker," I decided to alter the ad to read, "Opportunity to Learn The Business." Immediately, I began to attact and interview a different kind of applicant.

I had put myself in their shoes and thought, "What would I most want in being hired for a job?" My answer was an opportunity to learn all I could about a certain business. Instead of experienced sandwich makers, I now was attacting inexperienced, but teachable employees. I had always thought "experienced" was a given requirement. I was learning the hard way that a teachable, open individual made for a far better employee.

John Merriman came to work for us at $5/hour as a sandwich maker with a great deal of teachable spirit. When he left four years later, he was earning over $2,000/month still making sandwiches, but now managing the store. He had learned the business from the bottom up at a fast pace because he came with the specific intention of learning the restaurant business, and he did just that.

Finding a job and learning a business are quite different activities. Why not go for the whole works when looking for a job? It is simply a different way of thinking when approaching any employment opportunity.

"Opportunity to Learn" means I am open to all teachable humans with no discrimination except a closed mind. Wouldn't it be great if all companies and businesses had engraved over their corporate headquarters in big, bold letters, the words,

"OPPORTUNITY TO LEARN"

Asking For Work

Last week I hardly had any work. In fact, I only had one job and it didn't start until the next Monday. I decided to go out into some neighborhoods and ask if anyone needed work. This was something I had done when first beginning my painting contracting business three years ago.

The games I play with my mind are interesting, especially when I ring a doorbell or knock on a door. "They really don't want to be disturbed," "I might be interrupting someone," "They don't like salesmen," "They probably don't need their house painted anyway," "They are going to do it themselves." These were just a few of the thoughts crowded in my mind. In fact, the majority of the contacts are pleasant with the owner appreciating my concern for their property.

Within two hours one afternoon, I had received three bids totalling $3,000 worth of work. In another two hours, I went downtown to look at some buildings needing painting. In another hour, I had met an old friend who happened to own and manage ten other buildings, one of which I am bidding on this week. On another day, I talked with the managers of a large apartment complex who wanted all doors painted, 288 of them! They also wanted all trim redone with both projects providing a total of 30 days of work for three painters! Why is it I would rather do the work than ask for it?!

Perhaps when I have been accepted and there no longer exists a risk of being turned down, rejected, I can be more free to ask for the work. I feel so good when they accept my bid and I feel so down when I am not accepted. I wonder if I could also *feel* good when I am turned down for work?

Perhaps this is the real reason I would rather be *asked* than be the one doing the *asking. I don't want to be put on the spot.* If I go in with the attitude that my service is the *best* they could ever receive, and that if they do not accept it, the prospective client is the loser, then with this perspective, I could feel sad for the potential customer instead of feeling rejected myself. I wonder if the business realm would change in perspective if everyone asking for work who was turned down felt remorse for the employer instead of for themselves. This attitude would then place the *burden of service* on the person asking for the work.

Asking for Help At Work

Tom came to our meeting yesterday all fired up with enthusiasm and a notebook full of ideas. Tom is currently the manager of a Texaco station with 12 auto mechanics all working on straight commission. As a business consultant, I had asked all employees of the company in its four service centers how they would rate their current quality of customer service on a scale of 1 to 100. The answer was 80 percent. The managers decided that they wanted to see it improved to 90 percent.

The general manager, Tom, and I all sat down a week ago to create a one-hour idea session with the purpose of raising customer service by 10 percent. We had only one guideline: that all ideas would be accepted with no judgment as to their value. When we were finished, we had filled an entire page with a wide range of creative ideas. Tom was then asked to give a 10-minute presentation at the next manager's meeting on the subject at hand. I told him he had his presentation right there from this meeting.

The amazing thing was that he didn't present any of his own ideas, but rather went on for more than 30 minutes on the ideas suggested by the rest of his staff. All this after he had taken the time to ask for "help." The owner of the company was also present and got so excited that I had to stop him twice so we could just continue with the meeting.

What occurred here was so simple and basic but is something that is most often disregarded in a business setting, especially with men who know a lot about fixing cars! The owner had asked me for help. I had asked Mark, the General Manager for help, and then we asked Tom for help, who in turn had asked his mechanics for help. The result was exciting, enthusiastic, and rewarding to say the least.

Why is it that asking for help is so foreign to my nature? Why do I think I have to do it all? That if the world is to work well, I am the *only one* who can fix it! Maybe this comes from our ancient separatist view contradicting the truth that we are all *one* working together to make this world a better place to live.

Each time I ask for help, I am assisting in melting the barriers that separate us in the world. It might follow that when I want to solve any problem, my first thought could be to ask for help and then go to work. My normal pattern in the past has been to work myself into a hole and then, only when I've exhausted all my solutions, I finally ask for help.

Chuck Worthington, the owner of this company, is a wise man. He has learned to ask for help *before* he needs it.

The natural by-product is that he then creates in his business an environment for all the creative ideas of the his entire staff to emerge making his business the most profitable it can be.

Trust To Gain Freedom

What is my question today? What do I need to learn at this time? What am I most afraid to do today? Asking these questions on paper has assisted me in getting in touch with my feelings, opening the door to my next lesson in life. The answers always come when I allow the unedited words to be written by my own hand. Should I hire another person so I can go out and sell? I would rather hang on to what I have instead of adding another person to the payroll and then feel the pressure of needing to create more jobs. It is a matter of what I have as opposed to what I don't have — fear of the unknown. *I would rather be doing than trying to create more doing.*

I have prospects to talk to, but I put it off. Also, I put off calling people I've made bids to over the past year. If I were to do what I am afraid to do at this time, I would call another worker in and go with the unknown. In my business, the question is always, "Can I give better service by adding another employee at this time?

I just picked up the phone and called Jeff to come to work tomorrow. This will free me up to complete the bids I have in my file so I can then make new contacts.

I wonder if life is more rewarding when I do what I am afraid to do. It appears so on the surface. Does this mean I should put my life in danger or my emotions in danger by taking risks? Perhaps we are protected from this as I am never given a risk that I cannot handle. I must trust my own mind to give me challenges that are attainable without risk to body, mind, or spirit.

I wonder if taking on the smaller risks prepare me for the larger ones. Perhaps this is how I build up trust in myself to take the next steps toward *doing what I am afraid to do.* Trust leads to confidence leads to self reliance leads to freedom, which perhaps leads to *freedom from work.* Then it would follow that the more trust I have in myself, the more *freedom from work* I will possess.

Worry About Work—The Line Between Fearless and Fear

Today I have a significant bid to write up on a 256-unit apartment complex. This job entails painting all the trim on 25 buildings and painting all doors. Yesterday, I called Jeff in to work so I would have time for sales. In late afternoon, I received a call from a large company to give them an estimate as they had two and now needed a third.

It appears that the action of trust sometimes produces immediate results. One day I am feeling I don't have any jobs in the near future, and the next, I have more than I can handle. I also am bidding tomorrow on two houses that need work immediately.

Now I'm dealing with new fears. How will I staff these jobs? Will I bid them too low? Are the buildings safe to work on? Will the client pay me on time? Will the weather cooperate? How will I spend the money? Will the color match? Will we finish the job on time? Will I be able to take care of my present customers?

All this takes much trust in myself. Perhaps the only sane way to accomplish a large project such as this is to take it one step at a time. Translated this means staying in the present while at the same time planning out a future strategy.

How does one stay in the "Now" and also plan for the future? This is another of life's many paradoxes. When planning for the future, I must think of all the variables. What can go wrong or perhaps, what are the potential problems not obvious to me at the present? I need also to factor these into my bid.

Maybe if I focus more on being present and keeping my mind on accomplishing the bid, I can get through it without a great deal of worry or anxiety. Worry and fretting about what might possibly happen never seem to accomplish a thing. I have never met anyone who didn't worry, so it must have some purpose in the larger scheme of things.

Perhaps "worry" helps keep me in balance. I seem to need equal amounts of fearlessness and fear to walk the path of success. It could follow that success just means staying alive and letting the world know who I am while staying on the path long enough to allow this to happen.

The line between fearless and fear becomes finer and finer.

Mirrors in the Work Week

I had three significant meetings which were the highlights of this past week. I would refer to them as mirror meetings. I really get a good look at myself when I have an intimate communication with another individual. I make a point to schedule these sessions in my life, otherwise they never happen. They serve to keep me conscious, present, and remind me of who I am and who I am becoming.

First, I met with Lonnie, who runs a growing communications business that has doubled in size since we last met one year ago. I told him at the end of our two hours that I learn a great deal about myself each time we get together. Now we talk about almost everything except business.

One day, we were talking about ways business executives could stay in touch with the present moment. At that point, he got up and went over to smell a rose on his desk. "I do this almost daily. I take time to smell a rose. Why don't you come up with more ways that we as business professionals can create a 'now' moment?"

My lunch with Jeffry Meyers lasted another two hours, something we do every two weeks. Jeffry is a professional and an extremely creative photographer whom I have known since 1982. We usually talk about our projects, ideas about life and relationships, and our writings.

Both Lonnie and Jeffry are active listeners, a quality I am practicing more and more. My time together with people like this gives me another reflection of characteristics I am developing.

On Thursday evening, I met with my group for an hour and half. Here is one place I get wonderful feedback on my writings. Of course, the question always posed is, "What did you learn about yourself since we last met?" and "What are you doing to take care of yourself?" I look forward to this important gathering as I can express anything I feel like. If I have a discouraging day during the week, or if the entire week was a disaster, this is one place where I can tell the truth about what is going on, all of it. I feel more balanced after these meetings because along with the positive things, I have a place where the negative stuff, the darker side, is also given a safe place to emerge.

I guess I might say these meetings are *balancing-of-energy sessions.* Perhaps this is because so much trust is a required ingredient. In the everyday, fast-paced work world we live in, I wonder how many in our society schedule meetings with some person or group that we can totally trust, individuals who will be honest and clear mirrors of who we really are. Perhaps it follows that all destructive energy would be greatly reduced with such a weekly session. Maybe the growing number of therapists would soon be a "shrinking" number, no pun intended. The cost is only time, and the more I value my time, the more I seem to make time for intimate and open conversations with individuals I trust.

My first step is to ask who is interested in participating in open and honest discussions about Self-growth. It did not happen until I made the decision that this was important in my life. If one of my intentions in life is to know myself, I can think of no better way than to make room for individual mirrors with whom I can communicate on a weekly basis. These are individuals whom I can trust to be *honest* with me at all times.

This is the most powerful way for me to learn all I can about myself in an simple, inexpensive way. Today, ask yourself, who are your mirrors, those individuals with whom you have developed enough trust to be honest on a frequent basis about your own personal growth. What are other ways you have discovered to learn about yourself and enhance your own well-being?

A New Word For "Work"

What could be another word for "work?" There could be a word that conjures up word pictures other than those that are stress-producing. There must be a word or phrase for this activity of "work" that could denote a sense of freedom for a vast majority of us.

I was posing this question today to my friend, Jeffry, and he suggests we call this activity, "Love Vocation." When I say it fast, it sounds like "La Vacation," which feels and sounds much more relaxing than "work."

When I was an engineer at Boeing, it must have been stressful beyond my comfort level, as I used all sick leave built into the system. I also had many hours of "boredom," which is described as a "health care emergency" by Dr. Patch Adams, founder of the Gesundheit Institute in West Virginia.

When I was creating my restaurant concepts, on the other hand, I was seldom sick. I felt normal stress, but it was in my comfort level as I *loved* what I was doing, and that was my *only* motivation. I went many years without so much as a cold.

If what I am doing is "work," I can now switch to loving what I do and call it *Love Vocation*. If I can't honestly call it that, then I should quit doing it. This new phrase might just fit for those of us who honestly love what we do in service to others. *A Love Vocation* will not hurt me, will not bring ill health, will not push me beyond my comfort level of stress.

From now on when I work, I will ask myself whether or not this fits into my *Love Vocation* before I accept the job. If it doesn't, I will try to be strong enough to say "no," even if I desperately need the money.

Cynthia's Love Vocation

"I'll never work another day in my life."

Cynthia was running her own company when I began consulting with her in 1982 — a research group creating social impact studies for large companies and organizations.

I discovered she really liked the work she was doing and felt it was very important, but she felt it was hard work. She had accomplished a major increase in sales, a change of location, and a much better working relationship among employees, but for Cynthia, it all still felt like *hard work.*

As we met over the next 10 years, I noticed Cynthia began to shift from doing what she was "supposed to do," dictated by a Ph.D., to what she really enjoyed, which was primarily assisting others in the health care profession. In 1988, she selected a hospital organization she wanted to work with and became one of their administrators. About the same time, she began to explore and discover more of what she would love to do, even without getting paid.

Subsequently, Cynthia became a certified Doula, one who assisted mothers, alongside midwives, with birthing their babies. On many occasions, she found herself being called out of important meetings, but the hospital was understanding. A weekend retreat where she received a message that birthing babies was her number one reason for being here was the origin of a personal transformation process.

With no net worth, no college science courses and no nursing experience, Cynthia decided she wanted to become a midwife. With that choice made, the miracles began. First, she found the college that would complete her studies in three years. A friend then gave her $50,000 for tuition, not a loan, but a gift. Other friends sent her money for room and board various times just when she needed it the most.

In December of 1995, Cynthia showed up unexpectedly at our Christmas gathering where some 30 people shared their stories and passions. She had just graduated from the midwifery school at Yale University, and was now a certified nurse/midwife. At age 50, she had made a major life change. After relating her story, Cynthia shared a song with the group, something she had never done before, and later on whispered in my ear, "I will never work another day in my life." What she was saying was that, "I love delivering babies so much, I would do it even if I never got paid."

It appears there is a big difference between doing "work" and doing what you are passionate about. Cynthia trusted her passion and obtained freedom from "work" as a result.

Her story has helped me change so that I am asking the question, "What could I do for the rest of my life that will help my fellow man and love it so much that it does not matter if I ever get paid?" My own freedom from "work" will come from my exploring my own answers to this question.

Seven Kinds of Work

How many kinds of work are there? As many kinds as there are people. If we could categorize, they would look something like this:

1> *Work to Survive*
2> *Work from Guilt*
3> *Work to Prove Something*
4> *Work to Gain Power/Position (Greed Mixed In)*
5> *Work to Learn*
6> *Work to Express Creativity — Love Vocation*
7> *Work to Serve — Working to Have Fun*

Some folks work at “work” while others play at “work.” Perhaps even some get by at work, and then again, maybe some are working for the future. Some work hard just to gain sympathy from others.

I have done some of all of the above. My best choice always seems to be having fun at work — playing at work while serving to meet a need in a professional manner. Professional to me means the work is viewed by others as an honest endeavor, performed in a disciplined manner resulting in an excellent outcome. A satisfied customer is generally the primary evidence.

At present, we are not set up in our society to work at expressing our creativity, which, I believe, is our natural state of being. I wonder if the Universe is now encouraging us to do just that. It follows that those who want to survive would want to become aware of this form of work and pursue it *now*, rather than waiting for retirement. I know "standard of living" is at the forefront of our working society. Perhaps *quality of life* could move into first place. I could start with myself focusing on my *quality of life* as opposed to saving my fellow man. My willingness to focus on "being" can provide a model for others.

When I work to express my creativity in serving others, I am always having fun. It looks like play to me. It follows that my quality of life will flourish when I am having fun while expressing my own creativity in just "being" and serving others.

This is my *Love Vocation.*

Charles King has never worked a day in his life in the traditional sense. I suspected this as I was talking with his wife, Helen King, just yesterday about the very few individuals I know who don't work and yet seem to accomplish great things in their lives. Charles is as active today at 75 years of age as he was at 40.

I asked him if he has ever worked. "I can't think of a time," he answered. I responded, "You have a Love Vocation." He agreed — not only that, but his mission in life has been to encourage, sing about, talk about, and spread love wherever he goes. For quite a few years now, he has been the minister of The Musical Church in Bellevue, Washington.

I would definitely call Charles King a "love machine," someone turned on at the highest frequency wherever he goes. There was no job existing for what he does, no job description for this kind of so-called work. He created this job out of an intention to spread a message of love with no limits, boundaries, or dogma.

Mr. King directed the "Wings Over Jordan Choir" in the days of radio. As such, he traveled the United States singing spirituals in every major city. Every Sunday on CBS Radio, they performed to a listening audience of 50 million. What an experience for a young man fresh out of Julliard School of Music.

On March 20, 1994, the Charles King Singers, a reincarnation of the "Wings Over Jordan Choir," sang at the New Hope Baptist Church in Seattle, directed by Charles King. This was quite a unique experience in that we were an all-white choir singing original spirituals at a predominantly black church. As one of the soloists, I was moved deeply by the energy in the congregation and it was effortless to give my own presentation.

Part of Charles' mission is to build bridges and melt the barriers existing between our black and white cultural communities. This is definitely one powerful way.

Since I can't call what Charles does "work," there must be a different term for this. I wonder if just showing up with intention and purpose is all anyone needs in life. Perhaps I can trust enough that I will be taken care of in life, if I but *show up* fully with a purpose that will give me great joy. Charles King is a powerful model for those of us that want to be *free from work.* Charles King is one person who embodies the First Law of Money from Michael Phillips book, *The Seven Laws of Money.* "The money will come when you're doing the right thing."

Work to Survive

When I think of working to survive, I see pictures in my mind that depict humans planting and harvesting food so they can eat, building shelters for harsh winters, and making clothes to protect their bodies from the elements. It appears the work needed to survive is in direct proportion to that person's placement on this planet. There are areas on earth where very little work is required to survive as the area provides abundance in food and other items with a friendly climate requiring little shelter.

I wonder how many of us are still convinced we must work to "survive." I hear all the time how I must work to "put food on the table" and "keep a roof over our heads" as an excuse to get a job, any job. It's as if the people with work for us hold our very survival in their hands. Now some want the government to provide jobs for our survival! Did we forget that we are the government? It is not an entity separate and apart from you or me.

Perhaps it is up to me to discover the work that will give me the life style I choose to live. I do not recall a time in my life when I had to work to "survive." I wonder if this is true for the vast majority of people in this country. Perhaps if I take time to listen to myself and my own self-talk, I will hear the real reasons why I work. Maybe I don't work to survive after all. Perhaps it is a mere memory carry-over from my ancestors who dealt daily with genuine issues of survival.

Granted, there are even today, in the United States, cases of extreme poverty where in fact individuals are struggling for physical survival in food and safety. However, statistics as recent as January 1996 portrayed that the majority of households falling within the "poverty level" in the U.S., a category which qualified them for food stamps, medical, insurance, and many other benefits, had the following items in their household: VCR, television, computer, video games, etc.

Working to survive, for most of us in some countries, is so far in the past that it is a myth that no longer serves us. But what about the future? Shouldn't I be saving up for what can happen, a rainy day? Wealth is only temporary as we often see with money markets. Even real property can slide into the sea.

Perhaps the only work that can be recommended for the future is to educate myself. Education became virtually free to me since the day I received my library card. *Work to survive* is as outmoded as hitching up the horses to plow the field or going into town to buy feed.

Work Out Of Guilt

"Where are you working today?" "How much are you making?" Over and over again, I heard these inquiries from my fellow students following graduation from college and, in fact, for a considerable time thereafter. It was a most embarrassing time. I felt constantly that I should be working someplace else making more. The grass always looks greener somewhere else, especially when I'm working out of guilt.

Looking back, my response today would be quite different. Something like, "I'm not working and I'm enjoying life in this moment." Many of those not wanting to work found their way back to college for several more degrees.

In 1958, after working as an engineer for four years with Boeing and not enjoying it, I decided to go into business. Instead of informing my peers and parents of this new plan, I concocted a clever ruse, the brainchild of guilt, that I was going for my master's degree in business. Yes, this sounded admirable! I went so far as to sign up for classes at the University of Washington that spring and proceeded to carry 15 credits, none of which I wanted to do. I was digging myself in deeper and deeper, all because of guilt.

After completing one quarter of business courses, I decided to opt for the sting of guilt over the pain of more college, which by this time was considerable! I took the leap and went into business for myself for the first time in life at age 26 with no support from my family or peer group. I created a concept called "The Blue Banjo" in Seattle's Pioneer Square. It soon became one of Seattle's most successful nightclubs. Not only was I contending with my own sheer terror on a daily basis, but also the many predictions by friends and family that this would be financial ruin. In fact, an attorney friend of my family was asked to dissuade me from this certain disaster! Everyone was convinced I had departed from my senses.

Shame and guilt were my constant companions. It was truly one of the most difficult and challenging times of my life. To this day, I'm not certain how I was able to accomplish all that I did, especially with no support system whatsoever other than my partner, Joe Rutten, who was as terrified and inexperienced as I. Even now when I consult with individuals moving through transitions in business or career, I encourage them to never make any major leap as I did without setting up some kind of significant support group. It is always a wise thing for risk-takers to find other pioneers as support during those times of feeling lost, scared, and while you're being shot at by all those awaiting your failure!

I can always tell when I am working out of guilt. Today, the guilt issue still comes up from time to time. The phrases like "need to," "have to," and "should" come up in work situations, and on occasion even now, I work from that motivation.

My conscious choice, however, is to work to serve others and only do the things I enjoy. When I slip out of this place, I find myself getting stuck in an old muddy path — *the road to guilt.*

Work To Prove Something

It was just before Thanksgiving, 1958, and I was lying in bed at Virginia Mason Hospital thinking, "I've got to get out of here!" My first business venture was on the doorstep of opening the following Wednesday evening. I was feeling I had to prove that I could make it work. I was the only one who could do it! What eluded me, even as I lay in the hospital bed, was that the reason I was in this predicament in the first place was because of this kind of thinking.

I had been feverishly building a sign for the outside of the "The Blue Banjo," and without much effort, managed to blister my right hand. Well, that wasn't bad, but then I proceeded to get paint and turpentine in the blister. My hand became quite swollen, but I just ignored it and kept working. Well, that is until my hand wouldn't function any longer. When I finally got myself to a doctor, I learned he was immediately calling in one of the finest hand surgeon's in the city to operate first thing in the morning. It finally hit me that this was serious and that I could have lost my right hand, all because I felt I had something to prove.

I still have the scars on my hand as a reminder. But it took another ten years before I quit driving myself working in this manner. During this next decade, I would continue to say to myself and others, "There is no one who can outwork me!" This served me in a peculiar fashion as I tended to attract and hire workaholics. I would then secretly compete with them, all the while letting them think they were working harder than I. Deep down I *knew* that I was *the one* who made things happen all because of *my own hard work*. I put many hours in at home and then continued at work when the others were not there.

In 1965, when my partner, Joe Rutten, and I opened our ice cream parlour restaurant with 40 employees, we used to brag how many hours we put in each week. Joe and I grew up with the same work ethic in Minot, North Dakota, living only one block apart. One week he would work 80 hours a week and I would then work 108. The next week we would reverse the roles with me putting in the 80 hours while he did the 108! This was work-ethic heaven!

Looking back now, I wonder if I wasn't slated for early retirement due to health reasons. I am honestly not sure if I'd be around today if I had not decided to change my way of living. Without thinking, I shifted from *work* to *prove something* to *work to gain power,* the next category I will explore with you. Not much improvement.

I know this for certain. I still have this old desire to prove my worth, my intelligence, my skills and abilities, through hard work, and by being in demand in the marketplace. Thank God, it is no longer my major focus. Since I usually teach what I am here to learn, this will probably be one of the main things I will be teaching on this planet.

Work to Gain Power/Position

This category of work really serves the people who need to control their lives, others, and everything around them.

In 1973, I definitely needed to prove something. I left a partnership in a successful business that I didn't perceive was going anywhere. At least I thought it wasn't going in the direction it should. I developed and opened a 300-seat restaurant in Seattle called "The Breadline and Soup Kitchen" with the intent of selling the business in a few years for two and a half million or more. I sold it in one year for one and a half million. I was going to retire, never to work again.

I had graduated from "work to survive." I now had a mortgage on my home and a family to feed. "Work out of guilt," "work to prove something," and "work to gain power and position with greed mixed in" had all come to be my primary motivations in the marketplace. Here we were serving thousands of people every week and filling a great need. We were employing mostly senior citizens, and serving homemade soups, stews, breads, and pies at very reasonable prices with decor from the depression era. Then I definitely saw an opportunity to "cash in." Forget about our customers and employees, forget about serving the community with great food and all the senior citizens we were employing. Forget everything else except the dollar signs in my head and the opportunity never to work again!

Did it work? No, thank God! *Whenever I make a decision to do anything for the money, it never works for me.* I have bought several businesses and made many investments along the way, all with the intention of making money. To date, they have all lost me money and other valuables like marriages and friendships. Whenever I create a business to serve some need in the community unencumbered with the motivation of making a whole lot of money, or gaining power or position, I am always compensated with abundance in every way, including financially.

I do not know where I would be today if the business I sold in 1974 had been truly successful; if I had continued with a motivation of being of service to the community. The parties who purchased the business tried to squeeze even more profit out of the operation. Within months, the customer count was down by half and in less than five years, the business and the concept were gone without a trace. I received little more than token monies, slightly more than 10 percent of the contract.

A great lesson was given to me in this experience. If my intention going in was to create a business to serve without thought of retirement or cashing in on my creation, I have no doubt it would still be thriving today. I wonder if my own work intentions and outcomes are the same for others as well. When my intention is to serve, I always seem to have a positive outcome.

Work to Learn About Life

I think the most discouraging thing in life could be to work for 40 years for myself or someone else and then look back, defining this activity only from the perspective of what I outwardly achieved rather than what I was able to learn about life. More importantly, what I learned about myself.

Don Burke came to work with me two years ago. He had been by society's standards, a successful businessman, a lawyer for more than 13 years. After working different jobs for four years, he decided there was more to learn in the painting business.

I didn't think he would last long, as he had never done any blue collar work like painting houses before. He assured me he was a fast learner, so I paid him more than he was worth to me as an employee at the time, $10/hour.

Don left the law profession for several reasons. One was that he experienced the business of law as a game where there always needed to be a win/lose situation vs. a win/win. Perhaps there is more to learning about life or oneself when you know you can take care of yourself on a day-to-day basis. I know this is true for me. Don changed his name to "Sundance Burke" as it seemed to fit more with his life's current purpose. On each job, we not only discuss how we can help each client with painting needs, but we also assess what we individually can learn from each situation, each client. This kind of work, painting houses, lends itself to many learning situations, if I but pay attention. My office and my life's classroom, is presently a different person's home and property each week. I am entrusted with the keys to a client's home, an intimate expression of their life. I can now tell how a job will go by the energy in a home. It's amazing what a garage or carport can tell you!

We recently refused to paint the inside of a house because the energy between the couple that owned the home was fragmented with constant tension and no feeling of alignment or support. We really needed the work at the time and it was difficult to turn the job down. We are learning more to work in harmony not only with each other and our environment, but also with our clients. When we complete a project, we are always asking ourselves, "What did we learn on this job?"

When I show up fully and pay attention on each job, I am involved with *Work to Learn About Life*. This is a high calling.

Work to Express Creativity

It was April 1977. I can recall the conversation vividly to this day. I had just opened my new restaurant, a place where I could eat fast food that was also nutritious and healthy. Sitting across the table from me over lunch was an old friend, Dick Fike. He said to me, "You know, Jack, you are the most creative person I know." Now others had told me the same thing over the years, but this was the first time I had really heard this statement and acknowledged it with "Thank you."

For two decades now I had been building restaurants and expressing my own creativity in that way. I didn't realize until this moment that I would have done the same thing even if I never received a dime. I realized I was living my Love Vocation. I didn't consider this to be work in the least. Needless to say, the business was highly successful and I made money the first day we opened our doors.

A few years later, I invested $10,000 into a run-down restaurant with the idea of receiving a return of double or triple my money in three years. I was convinced there was no way we could lose, as my partner had agreed to work hard in fixing up this business. I knew we would end up making big money! Wrong again.

Every time I invested to make money, it didn't work out for me. I lost all I put into it and then some. This occurred three times in my life with restaurants alone. There were countless other investments, also failures. Perhaps for me, I can count on a healthy business that will support me with the profits *only* when I create it from the motivation of allowing my creativity to be `expressed to the highest degree. With this purpose, work was never work, but total fun. Unfortunately, I do not know many individuals who use their creativity to the fullest, which is a sad state of affairs.

I wonder if this can be accomplished on a conscious level. I know that for me it was primarily unconscious. One thing I did know for certain was that I didn't want to go back to the career I had had as an engineer working at Boeing. Creativity is frowned upon in most large companies. I did always move in the direction where I loved the challenge of creating something from nothing. Others perceived this as terribly risky, but I saw no risk whatsoever as I was consumed with enthusiasm and doing what I loved to do. After all, what did I have to lose?! Nothing from nothing leaves nothing! I ended up with many valuable experiences teaching me what does not work. This is exactly what a scientist does daily.

Perhaps being a scientist in business is the most creative act I can be involved in. *Work to express my creativity* can be the most important learning experience of my life if I only recognize and take advantage of the opportunities to do so.

Work To Serve

"What kind of work do you want to do?" " What are you going to be when you grow up?" A doctor, a mechanic, an engineer, a fireman, a teacher, a nurse? There are a wide range of established professions in which you could be of service. When I was young, what if I had said, "All of the above and then some." What if I had said, "I just want to be me and it doesn't matter what I do," or "It's not so important *what* I do, but how I can best serve my fellow man." What a concept! How it would be music to my ears to hear this response from young people today. I wished I would have said it a lot sooner!

The pressure to decide on a career or vocation was awesome when I approached adulthood. I had no idea I could look at the world and say to myself, "I will use my strengths, my talents I came to this earth with to assist my fellow man where I am needed most." Sounds a bit like Mother Theresa, doesn't it? Perhaps there aren't many of us in that frame of mind. Suppose we all were asked by our parents and teachers what our natural strengths, loves, and abilities were, and with them, how we might fill a need in our community? The educational system would transform overnight. Maybe it would cease to exist completely as we know it today. Our teachers can be the initial mentors serving our planet in this way. Maybe that is what is happening today. I for one intend to model this kind of mentoring that *works to serve* and assist at least one other person in learning how to serve wherever it's possible with that person's natural gifts and skills.

Work to serve seems so far removed from today's business consciousness. However, I do believe making this shift is essential for the survival of our planet. It is no secret that Mother Earth is no longer, nor ever was, the unlimited space we once perceived it to be with boundless resources. The only unlimited resource still untapped today is our individual desires and abilities to *serve each other.*

I wonder. Is this concept possible?

Soul Work

I have just listed seven kinds of work. I believe there is a new kind of work asking for greater emergence in the late 1990's called "soul work." I consider this to be the most important and powerful work we will ever accomplish.

During the early 1990's, we saw several books emerging into the mainstream to the great surprise of the authors, specifically *Seat of the Soul*, by Gary Zukav, *Care of the Soul*, and *Soul Mates* by Thomas Moore, and *The Heart Aroused*, by David Whyte. These contemporary authors all address the acknowledgment, care of and integration of the individual, cultural, and community soul back into every area of life. Since they have been so well received, it is probably time for a book dealing with *Soul Work in the Marketplace*.

It is a much different approach to work than we have experienced to date. Previously, our work has been based on our five senses, and it has served us well. Perhaps too well in that it seems to have overtaken the majority of us to the point of our own self destruction without many of us even noticing our personal demise.

I wonder if it is our attachment to money and stuff that serves to keep us in denial concerning our "work addiction." In my own experience, I do not want to give up my attachments. After all, they provide me with a great deal of security and comfort. Attachments seem to camouflage my "work addiction" and in turn, keep me from "soul work." Working from the soul or "soul work" is not about working on the soul. It simply means your work, your service, originates from a different place. Why not come from my Center, my Truth, my own depth of knowing when I do my work, if there is such a thing as *doing work*. Perhaps *being work* is closer to my truth.

Working from my soul, the center of my being, relieves me of worry concerning the future. It frees me up from the activity of saving, of hoarding, and from that most disguised of all diseases, "Earning-A-Living Addiction — Greed." I wonder if I could come from a soul level, if there is such a level, each moment I am engaged in "work." It follows that *work* could cease to be work. In short, *Freedom from Work.*

Work From Fear

Perhaps work is work when I work out of fear and work isn't work when I work out of joy.

All of a sudden, it is June 8, 1994. This should be the busiest time of the year for me, workwise. I was totally booked up painting homes in April and May. Now I have three employees working with me, fully trained, and no work.

What are my fears?

- *My workers will go elsewhere if I don't provide jobs for them.*
- *I won't be able to make the house payment this month on time.*
- *The money for vacations this year will come from monies earned between June and August, and there won't be any funds.*
- *The extra funds to get through the next winter are made during the summer, and there won't be enough.*
- *I'm 62 years of age, and I don't have any investments for retirement.*
- *What if I have an accident? I don't have a company that will support me as I had with the restaurant business.*

- *No work means I cannot keep my financial commitments and my promises to pay.*
- *I just found out I owe the court $1,000 more than I had sent them and my Chapter 11 bankruptcy will not go through until this amount is paid.*

One thing I am thankful for is that I am making fewer and fewer promises, which translates into less pressure for me. Some of my fears originate from my existing promises such as signed business loans using my home as necessary collateral, signed leases on equipment, and credit cards with high interest. I wonder how many people in this country are working out of fear for some of these same reasons. This often results in compromises that affect our well-being in the future.

I can remember when I worked at Boeing. I didn't care that we were building the B-52 Bomber, a weapon of mass destruction, even though there was no war. All I knew was that I wanted job security, a place to work, to be wanted and needed, to feel good about myself, even though what I was working on could destroy entire nations if it fell into the wrong hands.

I have often said that what I fear most is my next assignment. This doesn't mean I should work out of fear. Rather the opposite. Perhaps I should abstain from working whenever I have a fear that is motivating me to work. Then I might end up working only 20 percent of the time. What a scary thought! This means that 80 percent of the time, I would be working to get rid of my fears. I've just described an addiction.

No wonder the vast majority don't want to look at the way or the why of our "work." When only 10 or 20 percent of a population has an addiction, it will not get much attention. However, help is on the way. When 80 to 90 percent are suffering from an addiction, we are getting closer to giving it the attention it needs. Initially, the vast majority of individuals are going to have excuses and justification for their work addiction, regardless of its destructiveness to our environment, our health, our families, and our relationships.

Even with my growing awareness, it is easy for me to take the most lofty of service goals and transfer all my work addiction behavior to that new activity. Perhaps even some of our spiritual and "success" gurus are camouflaging "workaholism" as well. I know it is difficult for me to confront a "work addict," even someone I know well, because by ignoring that addiction, I am also protecting my own work addiction, past and present.

I can give reasons all day long why I work, and my excuses all ring with lofty-sounding platitudes. After all, my justifications are supported with hundreds of years of input. I am able to quote all the experts on why I should work and why I should work hard. "Work is a virtue." "It builds character." "I need to work hard in order to compete and survive in today's world." I am an expert on work, but I am a novice when it comes to not working. Perhaps my challenge for the remainder of my life here is to live in joy with no fear while not working.

If everyone worked only when the element of joy was present, rather than working motivated by our fears, what kind of world could we create?

A Working Day — When Life Is Going Well

Today my truck is working, my body is working, my life is working; life is purring right along. This is a time when I remind myself to notice when life is smooth as opposed to bumpy. Both situations are invaluable, but my real discovery came when things were rough just a matter of weeks ago. That was when I noticed things much more keenly.

I can now see how important it is to be in touch with my feelings when I am experiencing a very rough and rocky period in my life. Two weeks ago, nothing I did seemed to work out. I was overdue on my mortgage, I was asked to return and make repairs on a job that was already completed in my mind, and I couldn't get a new painting contract no matter how hard I tried! Staying in bed looked like the best alternative! If I hadn't faced the dark side of life, I know this wonderful day, like so many others in the past, would have slipped by unnoticed.

What is in my heart today? I can explain it from the outer results in my life. It is as if Spring has burst forth with abundance. First of all, my relationship with

Jane, my wife, is at an all-time high as is our parenting relationship with our son, Jason. Secondly, all of my work relationships with my fellow painters are exciting and rewarding. Thirdly, the environment I am working in, serving in, is probably the most beautiful around. And finally, the clients we are serving couldn't be more pleasant or pleased with our work.

I can now balance out my awareness and pay equal attention to the smooth life along with the rough times. If I give greater attention to the beauty all around me, I will create more thoughts of that grander nature within. It would follow that my outer world improves when my thoughts are raised to the level of the quality of life I wish to express.

Which comes first? My noticing or my thoughts? Does noticing the beauty around me create exquisite thoughts, or do the thoughts I entertain each moment create the environment I notice? "Being aware" is an event occurring in both arenas simultaneously. If there is no such thing as "time," it doesn't matter then which comes first. One awareness is evident. All my senses belong to the Universe.

"Your Presence Is Enough"

My friend, John Davis, made the statement, "My presence is enough," during the first of my eight-week "Money Unlimited" seminars. From then on, I made a point to integrate it as a primary focus in every class. It made quite an impression on the participants over the 70 plus seminars I co-conducted, with Sheila Connor, and later with my wife, Jane Bakken.

In every work situation and especially when applying for work, this statement, along with the mental image it conjures, sets the stage for *who you are* as opposed to *what you do*. In my own case, I have used it numerous times when preparing for a meeting that I might be anxious about. It means I don't have to do anything. I am already enough.

"Why do you think you should have this job or this work?" most potential employers ask. Rather than defend myself or list all my achievements, I could simply respond, *"Because of who I am."* In some cases, this will end the interview. If not, then the next question from the interviewer should be, *"Well then, who are you?"*

Now instead of stating what I do, which can get boring, I can express who I am, which is always more exciting. The strengths and talents I bring to this work along with my attitude and personality is what will make me valuable to any company.

Now I have created a much more vivid impression in this interviewer's mind. I will not be disregarded as just one of many. Knowing my presence is enough ends it right there for me. I don't need to go any further. My confidence shows through every time I use this statement with conviction. Every hiring company is looking for this in a potential worker, confidence.

It doesn't matter if the statement comes first or the confidence, as long as I get the job. Once I have it, I can figure out how to do the work just by being present. The first step in anything in life is *just showing up.*

"My Presence is Enough." I'll remember that again today.

Job or Relationships — What is Most Important?

Which is less important? Losing a job or losing valuable relationships?

Perhaps "work" is an addiction that should be treated just like an alcohol addiction. Many marriages are lost because of alcohol. I wonder how many marriages are lost to work. It doesn't seem appropriate in our society to sit down with a "workaholic" and confront him or her with this condition in the same manner as we would alcoholism. To work hard is to be respected and rewarded. Most companies love workaholics to the point of giving rewards to the individuals "who never missed a day of work in their life." "I haven't taken a vacation in 10 years!" Sounds like an addiction to me. "No," you hear the quick defense. "I really love my work!"

It is surprising how many put losing a job ahead of losing their spouse or other valuable relationships. If an honest survey were conducted, I would guess at least half surveyed would place their job close to, if not at the top of their list. And a "job" isn't even one's life's work or love vocation. A "job" is often an identity, a security place, a place to do, to perform, to prove.

I wonder how many children are being raised by "work-addicted" parents. Perhaps our entire society would be served in a more loving, caring manner if more people lost their "jobs." Again, I am not referring to those who are serving others to meet their needs. I am referring to the vast majority of our American society who have long left the survival needs and have lost their focus and priorities on what is truly valuable in life.

My friend, Mac, told me that he had had a heart attack some years ago from smoking three packs of cigarettes a day. It was this crisis that woke him up to the fact that he indeed had an addiction. Perhaps losing one's job would have the same effect on a "workaholic." I wonder if the downsizing being practiced by large corporate America will result in a much greater positive result in our society in the long run. Buckminster Fuller once said this about our society,

> *"One of the problems during the depression was too many people were working."*

Perhaps losing one's job could be the best thing that can happen to a "workaholic." This could provide the needed opportunity to explore the inner forces camouflaging one's work addiction, along with exploring passions, their unique abilities, and the ways to serve needs existing in the marketplace perhaps never before considered. Sometimes we focus on the perceived short-range suffering when there is often a far greater long-range benefit to be experienced.

Play

Is it true that many men don't play much as children and then grow up needing lots of toys and addictions to satisfy what they didn't receive? Interesting. Do we as humans always strive at some point in our life for what we never received in younger years?

If a child receives only serious messages from adult models and begins to work early on, perhaps the childlike nature isn't allowed to bloom into maturity. I define this type of "work" as both responsible work and irresponsible work. It can be delivering papers or delivering drugs. My own experience with childhood-deprived grown-ups is that they generally are high achievers with many adult toys. They appear to be very unhappy. The energy around them is usually anything but peaceful.

How can I as an adult recognize if I missed out on a part of my life and then make a correction so I do not become psychologically damaged? Perhaps I can start by asking myself how much my attachments mean to me. On a scale of 1 to 10, with 10 being the highest, what does my boat mean to me, my car, my home, my property, my membership in the sports club? It appears that a vast majority of humans in American society didn't spend enough time playing as children. We might refer to our social culture in the United States as "The Robbed-Children's Society." Perhaps 200 years of not enough play before the age of twelve has diminished our *childlikeness* as a culture.

I wonder how things might be different today if much more unsupervised play had been allowed. After all, it is the adults who allow or disallow free play. I have this tendency to want play to be a "learning experience" for my five-year old. I constantly find myself with feelings that it's time he grow up, mature, and keep up with the other children. If I can back off and allow him to be in his own world, perhaps I can practice entering his play world instead of insisting that he play in mine. Perhaps then I could learn to be at play rather than *play to learn to grow up*. He is teaching me.

Hard Work

"Man was born to be rich or inevitably to become rich through the use of his faculties." Ralph Waldo Emerson said this almost two hundred years ago. Notice, he didn't say *through* hard work.

When Thomas Edison said his work, his inventions, were 10 percent inspiration and 90 percent perspiration, we all believed him. Why? Nikola Tesla, an immigrant inventor of many electrical devices, who was considered by many as brilliant as Edison, if not more so, did not subscribe to this nonsense. Tesla was responsible for patenting the alternating-current motor and its subsequent sale to George Westinghouse, who in turn made it the foundation for the Westinghouse power system.

In spite of his genius, however, Tesla was ostracized by the captains of industry and money lenders. I believe the primary reason was that his inventions and the abundance of energy they would create for the common man for little or no cost would have led to masses of people not needing to work. Industrial and financial leaders were willing to do whatever it took to prevent this from occurring, and they did. Funds necessary to pursue development and patenting of his inventions were frozen and doors closed. Other scientists and inventors, even those living today, speculate that if Tesla had been given the open doors necessary in terms of funding and support, he would have been instrumental in ushering in an age of cost-free energy accessible to every household.

More recently, in the past 40 to 50 years, R. Buckminster Fuller, known as the inventor of the Geodesic Dome, met with the same resistance. His ideas for inexpensive, assembly-line housing was resisted by the building industry. He proclaimed that one of the biggest problems of our great depression was that, "too many people were working." I now believe what he meant was that when you are working, you are not inventing or discovering, and all you can see is what is staring you in the face — a pile of more "work" to be accomplished. Where then is the room for creativity?

At this time in our history, the once domineering corporate leaders are now seeking that inventiveness, that creativity, while in the same moment stifling it with demands for hard work. It's like trying to mix oil with water. Inevitably, one will sink beneath the surface of the other and remain there.

In his most excellent book, *The Heart Aroused,* (1994), David Whyte tells us there are elements that keep us from our creativity in the corporate world. They are just below the surface and scare the "Hebe Jebe's" out of us. These are the repressed monsters in all of us. The ancient tale of Beowolf is a masculine story of descent into the waters of the unconscious, and the restoration of a profound inner feminine power essential to a male's survival. He illustrates:

> *What are the modern corporate equivalents of these repressed monsters writhing just below the surface of our professional life? We can list a few of many. Most important: unresolved parent-child relationships that play out our rigid company hierarchies, paternal management systems, and dependent employees; unresolved emotional demands individuals may have of fellow workers, but will never admit to themselves; the refusal to come to terms with an abused childhood; the subsequent longing for self-protection and the wielding of organizational power and control at any cost to gain that protection.*

He goes on to say:

> *Perhaps the parent of all these vulnerabilities is Beowolf's mother herself, the deep physical shame that we are not enough, will never be enough, and can never measure up.*

Perhaps if I could always remember *My Presence is Enough,* then I could face my demons just beneath the surface and be warrior enough to take on all the advocates and addicts of hard work and say enough is enough! After all, hard work was my invention, not God's.

Back in June of 1994, during a time of my own development, I was facing my own monsters: I had a court date in July on my bankruptcy, my work had floundered, I couldn't make any payments, my wife suggested perhaps we look at divorce, and I had a sinus condition so bad I could hardly concentrate.

At that time, the following actions were on my mind consistently: I could stick my toe in the abyss, I could back away, or I could jump in with both feet. It wasn't up to anyone else. Only me.

As I look back, hard work did not save me, as I believed it had in similar situations. Instead I decided to jump in with both feet and live each day fully in the moment. I discovered this made it all worth while.

Scheduling No Work

Ever since I received my Day Timer back in 1972, I've never been without it. I have become an expert at planning what to do way ahead of time. Yet all my planning is around work and work-related subjects.

Most of my goals have been around money. Sell this, buy that, reach sales of this amount, and complete various projects producing income. It takes work to accomplish these goals. It also requires a lot of my energy. If the best way to take care of the people I love is to take care of myself first, then a change of strategy is in order.

Kenneth Axt, painting contractor in Woodstock, Georgia, works 3 1/2 days per week and grosses more than $400,000 annually. I work 5 1/2 days per week and gross half this much. Why is this significant? He is doing the same work I am doing. His story appeared in the 1995 Fall issue of a trade magazine called *Professional Painting Contractor.*

I decided to call and inquire further just how he accomplished this lifestyle. Most of the articles in the magazine are about how painters accomplish their work.

He said that the interviewer was far more interested in *how* he accomplished *so much* in such a *short work week.*

It all started with a goal to have time for himself. The article gives detailed information about what he does with the 3 1/2 days of work and not much about what he does with his other 3 1/2 days. Perhaps what is important here is not *how* he did it, but that he had a clear picture or goal of what he would do with the time not spent at work.

I was most impressed with his plans for Fridays. Friday is *his day*, not family time or time for work that spills over from the rest of the week. "This is my day off so I can sleep in, read, golf, lift weights, whatever I want." Saturday and Sunday are for the family. Monday is a relaxed day at the office with two to five hours spent at his desk.

I was inspired by Ken's story and thought if one painting contractor could do this, so could I. Last Friday, January 26, 1996, I had my first whole day for myself without guilt when I could have, "should have" been working. I spent two hours playing tennis in the morning followed by brunch with my friend, Jeffry, a long lunch with my daughter, Lorrie, and then a very restful afternoon with nothing to do! My goal this year is to have at least 20 of these Fridays off and in two years, no more work on Friday.

Re-thinking the 5-day work week is a big challenge considering the whole country seems to be moving toward a sixth day of work. In my painting profession, there are at least two people a continent apart modeling a different lifestyle.

Work is An Excuse

My pet excuse phrase is, "I love to work." It gives me plenty of avoidance material. Of course, I can easily get away with it in our American society. If "work" were labeled as an addiction, I would have to use a denial phrase. But I would still "work" in my mind while secretly reiterating to myself and others that I don't.

I think about work when the monthly bills start to come in, when I see some object that catches my fancy, when my wife wants something new, when my kids ask for something, when there is a pressing need somewhere in the world. I want to solve it with work to get money. I am a born problem solver and I can solve anything through my work addiction because money is the outcome of work in my society.

What if everything could be solved without money? What if no one received pay for *working*, but only for *being*? The more I could learn to *be*, the more I could have. Perhaps this is the way it is and we, the working class, don't seem to have a clue as to a different way to solve our problems?

At this time in my life, it takes a tremendous conscious effort to think of *not working*. *Being* doesn't seem to pay the bills, take care of my financial and other responsibilities, supply my family's needs, or my material wants. Maybe work is our biggest distraction invented by all of us so we don't have to look at "being" who we really are.

When I am really afraid to look at something, I create a distraction which usually becomes an addiction if I persist. So, I just keep telling myself and others, *"I love to work!"* even though it may not be bringing me any joy.

How Can I Support Myself?

I'm worried again. After a six-month run of continuous business, all painting jobs have come to a screeching halt. Can I support myself and my family through the winter months? I don't have a sense of freedom. What would give me a feeling of freedom? My mortgage payments for the next six months securely sitting in the bank would be the ticket! Support for me means having the mortgage taken care of. I wonder if most folks feel this way about their lives. I'm sure the ones still making rent and mortgage payments fall in this category.

How can we feel free enough to pursue our creative selves if we are always concerned about the rent? This society would probably be a more inventive, creative, and artistic lot if all *shelter and housing were of no concern.* A most preferable solution could be debt-free and rent-free housing. How do we get from where we are to that kind of life style? Do we even want to? Is it desirable? Sometimes I wonder as I watch others building bigger and more expensive dwellings increasingly difficult to pay for.

Under Communism, the people virtually had free housing. I do not advocate that kind of life style since the price is freedom. I believe it has everything to do with how we think. We can create an environment where we have freedom *and* no rent or mortgage payments if we can hold that vision. I look around and notice what the neighbors have or what my peers have, and I want that or better, even if it kills me! As a man, I say to myself, I want the best for my family. After all, I am the "Great Provider" and I would rather die than be accused of not being able to take care of my family in a manner consistent with my education and status.

It is interesting to me what I make important — standard of living, education, and health. Suddenly, I am thankful for my present condition of no work, as it has caused me to re-think what most of us don't want to consider: *Change*, a major change in our way of thinking and living.

The following project came out of this situation. My wife and I are planning to build a mortgage-free home using alternative building materials; a beautiful yet unconventional structure using straw bales for our main wall structure. It will be a Southwest-style home with an adobe look with over 2,500 square feet. The mortgage payments we are making on our present home will provide the cash to complete the structure in two to three years.

What would happen to our working lives if we could all be taught at some young age how to build our own affordable housing using available cash? Just think! Quite a number of the working class would need to work perhaps six months out of the year and use the balance to pursue creative personal endeavors. That is if the addiction to "work" could be addressed. Without going bankrupt, we probably would never have begun to entertain thoughts of how to build our own home easily and effortlessly.

Perhaps tough times for a majority of us folks would cause a re-thinking of our priorities. The choices we make evolving out of the tough times ahead are crucial to our evolution on this planet. They will be choices that have the ability to result in healing medicine to all of our social structures. It will be interesting to observe and be a part of this process.

"I Can't Find Work"

Listening to National Public Radio yesterday, I heard it once again, "I can't find work." A highly educated man with an MBA in business was being interviewed by Ray Suarez. The program was focusing on the job market and how many were unemployed. This man called in to complain that he wasn't even showing up in the statistics as his unemployment payments had run out.

One of the most painful experiences we as a society have created for ourselves is the idea that we must *find work*. More importantly, we *must keep our job* once we find it, at all costs!

The question is do we find work or does work find us? Sometimes the more I look, the harder I try, the more it doesn't exist! I wonder how many times this man has been asked to work on something and has turned it down because it didn't fit his personal job description.

I am amazed how much work there is out there if I just say "yes" to it. I am also amazed at how little work there is if I am particular about what I will do.

Perhaps work is a gift, a privilege, a reward, and the only way for it to serve me is for me to show up and be receptive. Gifts always come to me when I am willing to be vulnerable and open. Last week, a lady asked if I could build a room around her washer and dryer with folding doors as an access. It certainly didn't fit my job description, but I said I would get back to her with an estimate. Even though I had never done this before, I created a new room in this lady's home with which she was thrilled, and I made $400.

The only work I have turned down in the past year is when the values of the client didn't match my own values, which has been less than five percent of the time. I wonder if there isn't one person in my community who doesn't need some work done today?

From Pain to Enlightenment at Work

Speaking in front of more than two people was my greatest terror. I had already flunked the Dale Carnegie course. Each week, we got up and spoke in front of 20 people. Each week rewards were given to three or four participants. During the entire 14-week course, I had not received the smallest of rewards for my endeavors.

I had just opened my first business with only five or six employees. Having opened my second business in 1967 with 36 new employees, I was terrified to hold an all-store meeting. With the knowledge that we were going to grow to a staff of 300 to 400 employees eventually, I knew something had to be done about my fear.

I would rather have died than speak in front of a group and especially a store full of my own employees. They were looking up to me, and I was their terrified leader. They might discover I was afraid to stand up in front of them and give a presentation. Worse yet, they would find out I was stupid or didn't know it all! The pain was in my mind and yet I felt the suffocation physically!

I decided to go to Toastmasters, a choice I never would have made had it not been for my sheer terror around public speaking. Was having employees and going to Toastmasters part of my original destiny, or did I need painful or fearful experiences to remind me to grow? I'm still not sure.

Why is it *no pain, no gain*? Is this how the world is supposed to work? Did God set it up that we must suffer to evolve? Can it occur *without* hard work and *without* pain? Can we come closer together, help each other, love each other without *major calamaties* that in turn force us to get to know our neighbors, appreciate one another, and create powerful communities?

Is the birth of a newborn baby through much labor and pain our model for life? *Can we ever reach the point of spiritual gain when we don't have to suffer loss, rejection, accidents, so-called acts of God, and near-death experiences?* Does God do this to us or do we do it to ourselves?

Maybe we made a contract with God to live a certain way when we come to this planet and when we wander off this path, we are reminded by increasing degrees of pain how far we are out of alignment.

Perhaps enlightenment is sticking to our original agreement. Perhaps enlightenment is having a clear copy of the original and sticking to it. I wonder if they have Xerox's in Heaven? It sure would have made my life easier. As my good friend, Ron Connor, said yesterday, "Enlightenment is choosing growth when you don't have to."

Certainty at Work

Two days ago, a couple called, who had hired my services on several occasions over the past four years to paint and fix up their home. "We want you to paint the new home we just bought, and then paint both the interior and exterior of the home we are in the process of selling . . . and we'd like to start right away." Great news since I hadn't worked the week before and I had just received a letter from the IRS that they wanted $12,000.

I had ordered some of the paint and Sundance, my assistant, had already accomplished some prep work, which they had agreed to pay for. Other workers were to show up at 8:30 a.m., and we were to begin an $8,000 contract. Apparently, when the husband totalled up our bid, he went into shock and called the job off that morning.

Then at 7:30 a.m., my phone rang. It was my business phone so I thought, "Oh, good! Another client." On the other end of the line my current client said, "My husband says we should get three more bids."

It felt like the time when I was in college. I'd been so excited to get a job near campus drawing and designing bathrooms and other living spaces in a home. After three days, however, the owner came to me and said, "It looks like you don't have the skills to do this job and I'm letting you go." I was devastated. I had never before been fired from a job. Now, "three more bids" translated in my mind to "You don't know what you're doing, and we'd better get someone else to do the job."

I was moping around about two hours later when Sundance reminded me, "You know, Jack, the only thing certain in life is uncertainty." I acknowledged once again the truth of this hard-to-swallow life principle and decided to look at this experience in a different light. After all, I could have been in a violent car accident today or been informed that I had a terminal disease. In truth, this was a setback that was fairly minor.

Sundance then suggested that we write detailed spec sheets of everything we had bid on for the client and make three copies. We indicated the client's name at the top so the other bidders would know exactly what was involved in the project. This also relieved the client from requiring each bidder to measure the entire home, room by room.

I was not convinced that Sundance's idea was a good one, but when I brought the bid sheets over later in the day with the paint, the client was obviously appreciative, and said, "You know, we still want you to do this and we'll let you know what the other bids are so you can have another chance." *Uncertainty again!*

When I work for myself, I know I am asking for huge amounts of uncertainty. So, I am learning to welcome it, to embrace it fully, to allow it to enhance my actions. Uncertainty is what keeps me young and keeps me looking for miracles. I am never bored because I haven't a clue as to what might happen next in my life! Perhaps the day will come when I can embrace it sooner rather than later, even the moment it occurs. Without uncertainty, life would cease to be the exciting adventure that it is!

Work In Our Society

Work seems to have been invented by our society to keep the population in line and to keep the masses seduced into thinking they are happy. In fact, we are sold the idea that a happy and contented person is one who works. The dichotomy is that when men or women turn 65, they are perceived as less useful and need to be sold the idea of not working, hence retirement.

Interesting. "Work" seems only useful between the ages of 20 and 60, when I am perhaps stronger physically. But as I become wiser, more *knowledgeable and experienced* with years, I am then perceived as dispensable and not as useful anymore. As "Star Trek's" Mr. Spock would say, "Illogical."

It appears "work" is designed to keep me busy and out of the way for some forty years. Then a crazy idea called "retirement" will keep me out of the way again after 62. In contemplating this, what comes to me is the story related by Dr. Deepak Chopra of a sign that appeared below a picture of Karl Marx when the Berlin Wall came down — "Sorry, Chaps, it was just an idea." *

We as a society have bought this concept of work/ retire so fully that our whole focus of government is to provide jobs in the public and the private sector so we can all work. If one area moves out of balance, more jobs are provided in the other.

What is this kind of work? Mostly busy work. Oh, yes, productive in nature in that we must produce "stuff" that we so-call need. I wonder if even half the stuff in my home is "needed." I am told by advertisers, economists, and our government that if I quit buying "stuff," then the economy will drop and masses of people will be unemployed. I am also instructed to buy "American stuff." It is considered patriotic to keep my neighbor working so we as a society can *compete* in a global economy with the buying and selling of everyone else's "stuff."

Perhaps the world would work better for humankind if we quit competing and started to cooperate. There are good points in both Communism and Capitalism, but even with all the good combined in both, it does not equal the good that comes from Cooperation. If we could create and collaborate as varied cultures, each bringing our own

---

* Deepak Chopra is a medical physician considered one of the foremost pioneers in successfully combining eastern and western medical practices here in the United States. He is the author of fifteen books and more than thirty audio and videotape series, including the critically acclaimed public television show, "Body, Mind and Soul: The Magic and the Mystery. His works have been translated into twenty-five languages.

unique medicine, unique ingredients to the recipe, I have no doubt that we would end up with a much higher quality of life for *everyone*.

I wonder if a good close look at the three “C’s” mentioned might spring us from our prison and into the fourth big “C” — Creativity. I dare say that we as human beings are here to Create, not “work.”

Do Less

The less I worry, the more I seem to get done, although much of the time I am virtually doing nothing. Is this life's most hidden paradox? I have decided to try out the concept of doing less and having more. This is in direct conflict with the idea that "hard work is the only way to get there." Look at John Smith — "He put in all that hard work, and look where he got." Maybe John didn't work hard so much as he was focused on a particular goal. Just the idea of *focus* brought the goal closer.

It appeared hard work was the answer to achievement, but appearances don't always tell the truth. In my own history, focus brought me more accomplishment than hard work.

In 1982, I had a very bad knee. It was always swollen and for six months gave me much pain, especially when I played tennis. I was afraid I was going to have to give up my favorite sport. This problem received my full attention! The more I wanted it to go away, the worse it got. Trying to get rid of the pain through conventional means like physical therapy, chiropractic work, and other medical means didn't work. I decided to give it my full attention in another way and ended up creating a miracle with no hard work at all. Here's what happened.

I had just signed up for a five-week course on creating what you want in life. It was required that I select one problem or an opportunity to focus on each day. Twice a day for 15 minutes, I was to visualize the outcome I wanted while in a meditative state. For me, this was no easy task as I was not used to taking time out to do nothing except meditate. My preference was to *fix* anything in my life through busy activity, which I associated with hard work or to take it to a professional to make it work.

Nevertheless, for two weeks, 15 minutes, twice a day, I simply focused on what a healthy, flexible knee would look and feel like. After the two weeks, I was getting discouraged as I was still in pain. Yet, I decided to continue the focusing, which was quite a stretch for me. Half way into the third week, all symptoms vanished and my debilitating condition went away completely. I have not had the slightest twinge of pain in that knee since 1982. What I initially thought needed to be hard work turned out to be no "work" at all. It seems miracles can be easy!

You would think this would be enough evidence for me to religiously continue with this process with all my challenges in life. Not so! Old habits die slowly. So, here I am again looking at the concept of doing less and having more. I know focus and attention far outweigh hard work in getting what I want, yet I pick the latter most of the time. Why?

It is hard to give up what is familiar, especially when there are so many models of "hard work" and not enough models of the other. Giving my attention and focus to the concept of focus and attention and letting go of doing scares me although the alternative is to stay where I am. Change can be painful, but not as painful as giving up tennis or having a throbbing knee that doesn't work.

I am thankful that I am able to relearn again and again how my personal world works.

Retire At 62?

If my goal had been to retire at age 62, I would be in pretty bad shape right now. When I was 40, I was worth over a million dollars, and now that I am 62, I'm worth minus $153,000. If this were a medical scenario, it could be translated that I have gone from perfect health to fighting for my life with some terrible disease. Yet I am in great health now, and realize that net worth is only a bunch of numbers lined up on a page in a certain way. As is sometimes the case with a physical disease, I can reverse the cause of the financial ailment and alter the symptoms. It's totally up to me.

I have begun the healing process in my financial arena by focusing on what causes disease in the realm of money energy flow for me. I am realizing that some of the root causes of keeping money away from me are these:

1— Doing work for money

2— Not doing what I totally enjoy

3— Worrying about the future

4— Believing in hard work

5— Trying to keep up with others

6— Investing in promises of big returns

7— Investing in areas where I have little interest or knowledge.

8— Giving my power away to others in the area of money.

The discovery of the above for me has been the result of major lessons in my life. I would not trade any one of them for millions of dollars. Now that I know what doesn't work for *me*, I can now focus on total financial health. I can consciously explore what it looks like, how it works, and stay with the program that works for me. As each individual has a unique body and health system, each of us also has a unique financial and earning system, and both require care. I plan to treat my financial system as delicately as I treat my physical health so that I might become extremely healthy in all my financial affairs.

I can take each of the eight items I have listed above and turn them around to work *for* me. I have been a slave to them for so many years. It's now time I become *their* master. I hate to admit that denial on my part has kept me from looking more closely at each of the causes for my at-risk behavior when it comes to money. Self-forgiveness seems like a healthy place to begin and I know that I don't even need to do it all myself. There is an Infinite Knowing and Power greater than I always flowing in and through me. I wonder if I can allow more of that Energy Flow through my life even in financial areas by letting go.

It is a great time to be alive!

More Time for Myself

I have just spent the last eleven days with family and friends without working one single day. It was a wonderful, enjoyable, and peaceful experience. Amazing in that I currently owe about $4,500, more than my usual expenses, and the savings I had accumulated during the summer months are almost gone.

Despite all that, I discovered that living in the moment has all the benefits it promises. I could have had a miserable Christmas and New Year's if I had allowed myself to worry about my financial situation.

Instead of worrying, however, I used this time to focus on what I accomplished in 1995 and also to write it down. Then I focused on what I wanted in 1996 and also wrote that down. I then listed ten major goals that I wanted in the coming year, and made it OK if I just reached one of them.

Writing down my goals and accomplishments serves to keep me focused. It really helps when I am tempted by promises of quick and enormous returns by all the multi-level ideas friends keep presenting me with during the year. If a proposal is not in alignment with my personal list of goals, it won't receive my attention.

I remember times when I didn't have a very clear list of goals of what I wanted. Much time and energy was spent helping others reach their own goals. I believe all ideas are great and have their own purpose. My purpose is to be true to that which works for me, my own program. It's amazing how I can get off my planned agenda when a crisis arises. When this occurred in the past, I used to worry and fret, and before long, found myself way off course.

Each year gets easier as I learn to say "no" to others and "yes" to my own life's purpose reflected in the personal goals I set for myself.

Stand Still

In David Whyte's new book, *The Heart Aroused*, I came across a powerful poem dealing with the issue of waking up and saving our lives given by a Native American elder. The poem is in the form of a story, the kind an elder would tell to a young person whose life depended on the question, "What do I do when I'm lost in the forest?"*

Lost

Stand still. The trees ahead and bushes beside you.
Are not lost. Wherever you are is called Here,
And you must treat it as a powerful stranger,
Must ask permission to know it and be known.
The forest breathes. Listen. It answers,
I have made this place around you,
If you leave it you may come back again, saying Here.
No two trees are the same to Raven.
No two branches are the same to Wren.
If what a tree or a bush does is lost on you,
You are surely lost. Stand still. The forest knows
Where you are. You must let it find you.

---

* Poem has been translated into modern English by David Wagoner, Chair of Poetry, University of Washington.

The hardest work I do is non-work. Maybe I could call it "un-work." I feel I should do something. Others feel or say I should do something. The tax collectors tell me I owe money and that I should work more to pay them. Ever since our bankruptcy was finalized in January 1995, more and more non-dischargeable debts have been rising out of the depths to attach themselves to me and bring me crashing down.

Perhaps if I work harder, I can pull myself out of their clutches. This is what I have done in the past. So far, it has always seemed to work. Then again, maybe that is what got me here in the first place.

I don't have much energy to fight off the IRS and their claim for $11,000, the State Revenue demanding $8,000, Sea-First Bank's judgment for $4,000, or the SBA to the tune of $130,000. I do have the energy to build a new home, from the ground up, mortgage free, to write as I am doing now, and to paint houses, inside and out. It seems as though the business debt of the past will take forever to pay off at the rate I am going. Right now, I am paying $300/month to the first three creditors and the SBA owns all the equity on our home.

Is non-work the answer? It's so easy to focus on what I *don't want* right now and difficult to focus on what I *do* want. Is this a test for my self-righteous self, my ego?

If I stand still and listen without doing anything, will I be OK? The forest knows where I am. I must *let it find me*. In the past, I've persisted in getting lost, and I used my mind to save me. I realize now that this was only an illusion, and the real saving comes from my powerful self when I can stay in the present moment.

More "present moments" come from standing still. That's logical. But how do I make it real? Not by *thinking* about it. The whole world knows where I am. I must let it find me.

Vacation From Work

"Thirty-seven percent of the American work force did not take their vacations last year." This from a report I heard on one of the our reliable radio stations last week. I know some individuals have never taken a vacation, but I had no idea that almost four out of ten don't take time off every year.

My first thought was, "No wonder the divorce rate is so high in this country." It appears "work" is given a much higher position on our priority list than relationships. For me, I am now aware that one reason I persist in "work addiction" is to avoid dealing with intimacy issues with my family or anyone else, including spending time getting to know myself. It also makes it easier for me to avoid anyone holding up a mirror reflecting "work addict." Work is a much more comfortable and familiar arena to me, especially as a man.

Gary Smalley, one of America's gurus, shared how they did a study of hundreds of couples, and the number one activity that brought a family closer together was camping. Yes, *camping*! I didn't believe it myself. He explains how it is the spontaneous crises that occur in close quarters that create the bonding. Of course, no one appreciates it much during the actual trip. In fact, many swear they'll never go camping again! However, the benefits of the resultant comraderie are evident after the camping.

I would have to say the number one activity that *keeps* a family and other relationships *not working* is "*work addiction.*" This is not the kind of work we did hundreds of years ago in order to survive. Often that was like going camping; it brought people closer together. When families built a house or barn together, farmed or raised cattle, they would create a bond due to the shared experiences of surviving the struggles and hardships. In the 90's, the kinds of work we do, and the intensity and drive with which we do it requires most family members to be apart from each other for the major part of the day, week, and for some, month or year. Much more time is spent with fellow workers than with their own families and extended family of friends. Most certainly this is the case when travel is involved.

When my wife, Jane, says, "It's time to take a vacation," I immediately come up with ten, sometimes twenty, reasons not to go. "I don't have the time!" and right on its heels, "We don't have the money!" Vacations can be threatening! They mean time together which is unfamiliar territory for a large percentage of us. We might have to be still . . . get to know ourselves a little better . . . explore the unknown . . . talk about "issues" in our relationships. No! We're definitely not going on vacation! Perhaps we could just eliminate vacations altogether so most of us could feel safer!

Focus

In the early 70's, I created a restaurant concept that was so popular that most everyone around was talking about it. After we opened for business, I was completely exhausted. Yet, I cannot recall one person involved with the project complaining about how hard they worked, including me. For the six months prior to opening, I was completely focused on this project alone, sometimes working twelve to sixteen hours a day. I threw away my watch, literally, and for my partner, Bill Keegan, and me, time held no meaning while we were absorbed in this creative process.

Why do I hear repeatedly from folks, "It takes hard work. To accomplish anything in life, it takes work and not only work, but hard, hard work, and lots of it!" Does this sound exciting to you? My body feels the tension every time someone even makes that statement.

When I am doing what I love, what I enjoy, it's not hard work. When I am doing what I don't love, it's darn hard work. What's going on here? If I love what I'm doing, I automatically focus. I think most of us do.

It follows then that having a boss, a teacher, a peer tell us to "work harder" will have little or no impact. If I am having a good time, I will automatically focus on what I am accomplishing. Therefore, all I need do as a teacher or an employer is to create an environment for my students or staff that is supportive and fun, one where it is easy to learn and to ask questions, and to reach for the highest in themselves.

Focus is an automatic response to doing what I love. Hard work, on the other hand, has to do with should's, need to's and have to's, and actually can have a negative impact on my creativity.

I can also set up an environment for myself to create whatever it is that is valuable to me. What I want has often little to do with what I need or what I should do. Focus is focus, and I never need to trick myself into doing it. It always occurs when there is passion and interest, when I love doing what I am doing.

Passion

What if I were forced to choose between passion and success? To be successful or to be passionate about something? My first thought is that success is a barrier. It can get in the way of my passion.

"Success" appears to be an imaginary status imposed on me by the society we live in. I have a passion to be of service to humankind so all can explore and be involved in pursuing what they love. In other words, I want to facilitate others in living out their own passions. A large majority of people, men in particular, are not at this time pursuing their passions, me included. It comes up once in a while, but having a "successful" job, career, family, club membership, and financial security commands much of my focus. As a consequence, learning about myself and living my life's purpose passionately receives little or no attention.

In late September 1950, I entered Seattle University. I wanted to become an architect. Since no architectural school existed at that time, I was advised to take civil engineering to give me a stronger foundation for entering an architectural school sometime down the road. After all, architects were plentiful and if I wanted to be a "success," I was advised to become an architectural engineer. They were far more rare and earning higher income, I was told. Not once was I ever asked, "Jack, what is your passion?" And not once did I question this expert advice.

My guess is that the universities in this country are far more interested in showing off their so-called "successful graduates" in terms of how well they perform. In a sense, they have characteristics similar to that of multi-level marketing.

A multi-level recruiter once told me: "John Stickney makes $9,000 per month in his line of work. If you invest only half of that amount of effort in this multi-level plan, you will probably make $4,000 or $5,000 and still have time for your regular job."

What I wasn't told was that John is passionate about this work, and that *if I am not,* I should go elsewhere.

Well, now, I am not blaming the University or the multi-level recruiter. They didn't know any better even though I thought they did at the time. The change I would love to see come about, what I am passionate about, is for all young minds to be encouraged to pursue their passion and forget, yes, *forget about "success"*. Perhaps "success" is identified with the reaching of a goal, while "passion" is more concerned with the quality of the journey.

If I had to choose this day between reaching my goals and a passionate journey, my choice without hesitation would be the latter. I continue to discover that all the FUN is in the journey!

Freedom To Work

In 1975, Muhammad Yumus started arranging small loans for indigent people in Bangladesh. Today, the Grameen Bank he founded has loaned over more than one billion dollars to two million people. Nearly one-half of the bank's long-term borrowers, 46 percent, are no longer in poverty. Most of the loans are what we consider very small and made to women. The incredible part of this is that 98 percent of the loans are paid back.

What is going on here? These loans are going to the poorest of the poor. What does "freedom from work" mean to them?

What they do day after day is try to survive and stay alive. What little work they do find does not appear to serve them at all. Real work to them means some sort of income, and steady work means their standard of living or quality of life is enhanced.

Freedom from work only has meaning when an individual has work. Perhaps it is the same as fasting or tithing. First I must have enough food or money to begin either. What is it that in some places in the world there is an abundance of food, water, and shelter for the inhabitants, and in other locales, there is a lack?

Can this imbalance be solved and is it up to me to be a part of the solution? Perhaps if I could ask the person who has nothing what he or she really wants, then we could both learn something rather than persisting in my old approach, *fixing it* by giving food or shelter to the so-called needy.

If I were one of the poorest of the poor, perhaps the best way I could help myself is to help my neighbor who has as many needs as I. My contribution to humanity and to raise my own standard of living would be to fill the needs of my neighbor by producing whatever is needed using my God-given skills and abilities. At that point, my most pressing need would be the tools and the means to get started.

In 1963, my partner and I owned a unique ice cream parlour in the historic district of town. What equipment we had was old. The business was struggling, and we couldn't borrow any money. We had no assets. We decided to acquire some wisdom, as we were very young. So we asked August Pantagis, successful businessman and head CEO of our ice cream supplier, to meet with us for one hour once a week, for which we offered $15/per meeting, a huge investment for us at the time!

He said he would be honored to do so. Not only did he share his wisdom each week, but he also helped us find a sympathetic banker who in turn lent us $2,000 for new equipment. To this day, I would label this as one of the smartest decisions we ever made.

It is extremely difficult being a male in our society to ask for help and even more difficult to ask for a loan without the assistance of wise counsel. As the business grew and we paid back our loans, it became easier and easier.

If someone had merely given us $2,000 at the time or even co-signed a bank loan for us, we would not have gained the valuable experience we needed at that time.

I have a burning desire to help people that have a need to help others through their own enterprising spirit, but do not have the assets or means to continue or even get started. Perhaps the most harm I could do is to give these people food and money when all they want is to feel worth while. To be paid for serving your neighbor and then paying back a loan that got you started can only help to build self worth.

I support the model that Mr. Yumus started to such an extent that 50 cents from the sale of each book, *Freedom From Work*, will go to assist in the development of his discovery in our own United States where it is even more difficult to evolve this program. By purchasing this book, you have contributed 50 cents to organizations that are attempting to make this program successful in our own country.

Thank you for your participation in this work.

In Conclusion

My working hard is only a symptom of something deeper going on inside of me. I work hard to provide for myself and others. To store up money, things, food and shelter. I work hard to feel good. But the harder I work, the less I seem to accomplish this, so I end up working even harder.

I have this idea handed down to me over hundreds of years that to survive, I must work hard, and to have the good life, I must work hard in order to have a future for my children. I must work hard, individually. In order to raise our collective standard of living, we must all work hard. Therefore, I must *make sure everyone works hard* to ensure a prosperous future.

If I never look at what is going on with this story, I will just keep working harder and pass the myth on to the next generation.

It's time to *stop working hard* — to stop providing, to stop storing up for the future, to stop producing so we can all feel better. There just might be more to life on earth than to spend a lifetime becoming financially independent. After all, even if I am financially independent, what happens to those individuals who are not? If I become financially independent at the cost of one other person, I really haven't accomplished anything. Instead, I have created more misery.

Freedom from work can be simple. I wonder if I can accomplish it in my lifetime? I can start in this moment and grow into living that freedom for one day. That surely would be a big step.

Daniel Quinn notes in *Ishmael*,

> *Christ said, "Have no care for tomorrow. Don't worry about whether you are going to have something to eat. Look at the birds of the air. They neither sow nor reap, nor gather into barns, but God takes perfect care of them. Don't you think he will do the same for you? In our culture, the overwhelming answer to that question is, "Hell, no!"*

I work harder because I don't know how to *trust*. I don't trust any providential Being, or myself. So, I store up money, food, build shelters, and no matter how much I do this, I still never feel quite safe enough. So I escalate the process to feel better while the situation only gets worse.

This adds up to self-destruction.

So what is going on deeper in the scheme of things? That I don't trust God? That I need to be in control of my world, my destiny, my life here on earth? Perhaps if I trust more, then I will be *free of work.*

I Want Your Story

I want a short version of how you have created freedom from work in your own life. Edited selections will be published in my second book entitled *101 Stories of Persons Who Have Found Freedom From Work.*

Send your story to:
Jack Fecker
c/o Hara Publishing
P.O. Box 19732
Seattle, WA 98109

You will be credited for your contribution and will receive a free copy of the book.

Lectures and Seminars: You may contact me at the above address for speaking engagements and seminars on the subject of money or work.

ORDER FORM

Qty.	*Title*	*Price*	*Can. Price*	*Total*
	FREEDOM FROM WORK	$11.95	$14.95	
Shipping & Handling (add $3.00 for one book, $2.00 for each additional book)				
Sales Tax (WA Residents only, add 8.2%)				
Total enclosed				

Telephone Orders:
Call (800) 461-1931
Have your VISA or MasterCard ready.

Fax Orders:
(206) 672-8597
Fill out order blank and fax.

Postal Orders:
Hara Publishing
P.O. Box 19732
Seattle, WA 98109

Payment: Please Check One

☐ **Check**

☐ **VISA**

☐ **MasterCard**

Expiration Date:_______/_______

Card #:____________________

Name on Card:____________________

Name ______________________________

Address ______________________________

City ____________ **State**______ **Zip** ______

Daytime Phone(   ) ____________________

Quantity discounts are available.
For more information, call (206) 775-1481.

Thank you for your order!

I understand that I may return any books for a full refund if not satisfied